# Social Goodness

# Social Goodness

## The Ontology of Social Norms

CHARLOTTE WITT

**OXFORD**
UNIVERSITY PRESS

Oxford University Press is a department of the University of Oxford. It furthers
the University's objective of excellence in research, scholarship, and education
by publishing worldwide. Oxford is a registered trade mark of Oxford University
Press in the UK and certain other countries.

Published in the United States of America by Oxford University Press
198 Madison Avenue, New York, NY 10016, United States of America.

© Oxford University Press 2023

All rights reserved. No part of this publication may be reproduced, stored in
a retrieval system, or transmitted, in any form or by any means, without the
prior permission in writing of Oxford University Press, or as expressly permitted
by law, by license, or under terms agreed with the appropriate reproduction
rights organization. Inquiries concerning reproduction outside the scope of the
above should be sent to the Rights Department, Oxford University Press, at the
address above.

You must not circulate this work in any other form
and you must impose this same condition on any acquirer.

Library of Congress Cataloging-in-Publication Data
Names: Witt, Charlotte, author.
Title: Social goodness : the ontology of social norms / Charlotte Witt.
Description: New York, NY : Oxford University Press, [2023] |
Includes bibliographical references and index.
Identifiers: LCCN 2023013823 (print) | LCCN 2023013824 (ebook) |
ISBN 9780197574799 (hardback) | ISBN 9780197574812 (epub) |
ISBN 9780197574805 | ISBN 9780197574829
Subjects: LCSH: Social norms. | Social values.
Classification: LCC HM676 .W58 2023 (print) | LCC HM676 (ebook) |
DDC 306—dc23/eng/20230414
LC record available at https://lccn.loc.gov/2023013823
LC ebook record available at https://lccn.loc.gov/2023013824

DOI: 10.1093/oso/9780197574799.001.0001

Printed by Integrated Books International, United States of America

# Contents

*Acknowledgments*     vii
*Preface*     ix

1. The Great Puzzle of Social Norms     1
2. Social Role Normativity: Internalism and Externalism     19
3. The Artisanal Model     40
4. Social Norms and Social Reality     66
5. Habituation, Imitation, and the Critical Self     84
6. Self-Creation and Transformation     101
7. The Artisanal Model and Social Hierarchy     116

*Epilogue: Social Roles and Oppression*     131
*Select Bibliography*     135
*Index*     139

# Acknowledgments

The ideas in this book have greatly benefitted from conversation and discussion with colleagues and friends. I first floated the idea of habituation as a critical method at a conference on "Virtue and Moral Reasoning Under Oppressive Social Conditions" at Concordia University in 2018, and I introduced the idea of the artisanal model for social role normativity at the Critical Social Ontology Workshop also in 2018. It was very helpful to discuss the artisanal model at a colloquium at Wesleyan University in 2019 and at a Faculty Fellows talk at the University of New Hampshire in 2020. Finally, it was a great pleasure and very helpful to discuss my book with my friend Ásta in a conversation in the philosophy department at UNH, and with the SHAPE Reading Group at MIT during summer 2021.

Sally Haslanger and Joe Rouse have been trusted philosophical interlocutors and supportive friends on this project and I am grateful to them. Mark Okrent has been with me every step of the way. His unique gift of being able to enter a philosophical project and improve it was particularly useful during the isolation of the pandemic. And there is no one I would rather quarantine with.

I am very grateful to the Center for the Humanities at UNH for supporting this research with a fellowship in 2018. And, I also thank Dean Michele Dillon and the College of Liberal Arts for supporting the final phase of this project.

# Preface

One fish asks another fish, "How's the water?"
The other fish replies, "What the hell is water?"

We are all immersed in a sea of social norms, but they are sometimes tricky to observe with any clarity. Even though our daily actions, engagements, and reactions to others are conditioned by a web of norms, they are often invisible to us. Yet they are right there in front of us, as we will soon discover if we try to move too far from the norm or try to move away too quickly. The paradoxical fact that social norms are both invisible and all too visible is one source of their fascination for me. Not only is the ocean largely invisible to the fish who inhabit it, but it is both life-giving and enabling, and restrictive and limiting. Social norms are our ocean; they are the medium through which and by which we engage our techniques for being human. They are both limiting of our freedom and the conditions of our agency.

When I want to illustrate the topic of my book to an audience, I can simply refer to features of the present occasion: where the audience is seated; who sits at the seminar table; where the speaker stands; who talks and who is silent. Sometimes the audience silence is broken by a similarly choreographed question period with its own set of norms governing when and how various audience members ought to participate. Everybody in the room is responsive to these norms unless there is a rank outsider or newcomer present. No one is enforcing these norms; no one is telling anyone what they ought to do or ought to refrain from doing. As I said, often we are not even aware of the norms governing a situation. If someone speaks out of turn, however, or starts to talk on the phone or starts to sing, we are suddenly aware that a norm has been breached and that someone is not behaving as an audience member ought to behave. Apparently, our delinquent audience member did not endorse the norm or chose not to follow it. But what, then, is the source of that "ought to"?

One of the interesting things to notice is that the speaker norms cluster around or attach to different social positions or roles in different ways. The social norms that we are responsive to and evaluable under vary depending upon our identity or social position. If you are a student, perhaps you ought to ask a question, but you ought to ask it in a certain way. Be respectful. If you are a student there is a technique for asking a philosophical question, a way you ought to do it in a specific context. And you learn how to ask the question by watching and imitating others and becoming habituated into the ways of academia. If you are a professor, then you are responsive to and evaluable under a different set of norms for question asking. Perhaps the norm in this case is to be combative. Of course, both in the case of students and in the case of professors, the norms are slightly different yet again if you are a woman or if you are a racialized minority.

For me, the realm of social norms emerged in all its force and complexity when I was thinking about gender and gender norms in relation to a book I was writing. I was stunned by how much of my day-to-day existence was shaped by gender norms; including those I criticized and those I was not initially aware of. It became very clear to me that even my rejection or criticism of a gendered social norm presupposed in some way that I ought to follow the norm. And I was hard put to explain that "ought to," given that I rejected the norm. Social normativity is an important kind of normativity to understand, not just for me of course, but for all denizens of the social world, each of whom occupies and enacts a panoply of social roles. Think for a moment about how our lives are textured and given meaning by our social roles, on the one hand, but also limited and sometimes distorted by them, on the other. Both the empowering and meaning-making aspect of social roles *and* their oppressive and limiting aspect are essential parts of the story. And just as important as our ability to criticize and to reject norms is our capacity to modify or to change them. Underlying each of these parts of the story lies the central question of the source of social role normativity. This basic question determines both the plot line and the shape of this book.

# 1
# The Great Puzzle of Social Norms

"The great puzzle of social norms is not why people obey them, even when it is not in their self-interest to do so. It is, how do shared standards of conduct ever acquire their normativity to begin with? Once we understand this, there is no further difficulty in understanding the motive to obey them. We obey them because we believe that we *ought* to." (191)

Elizabeth Anderson

In *Social Goodness* I propose an answer to Elizabeth Anderson's question, "How do shared standards of conduct ever acquire their normativity to begin with?" This is the central puzzle of social normativity. As a mother, I *ought* to put my children first, but as an academic I *ought* to pursue knowledge above all. Where do these "oughts" come from? What is the source of their normativity? Are they different from ethical or prudential norms, and if so, how are they different? And why do they attach to me, seemingly independent of whether I subscribe to them? As Anderson says, our tendency to conform to social norms is a consequence of our recognition that we ought to do so; it is a symptom and not a cause. What then *is* the source of the normativity of social role norms?[1]

---

[1] I offered an early version of my answer to this question in my paper "What Explains Social Role Normativity?" in Hufendiek et al.

Before we begin to address that question, it is useful to pause for a moment to consider the significance and omnipresence of social roles. Let's consider the personal impact of social norms. We are often confronted with normative demands that appear to have a source external to ourselves. That is puzzling, because we also often also think that demands at the level of social norms are a matter of our own choices and preferences. After all, isn't it up to me whether I ought to conform to my culture's gendered norms of appearance or maternal norms? We might think the right answer to this question is that it is my choice and up to me to decide. Indeed, we might think that the only legitimate origin of normativity is the individual and her attitudes or preferences. But if so, then why do we so often find ourselves following norms that we don't endorse and of which we are critical? Thinking through the issue of the source of social normativity can provide a better understanding of our own normative situation, its inner contradictions, and how it works. Spoiler alert: Our preferences, endorsements, or attitudes are not the source of normativity of the social norms we stand under, or so I argue in this book.

In what follows I am particularly concerned to understand two things. First, what is the source or basis for social role normativity? To borrow a handy term (Brennan et al. 24), where does the normative "oomph" of social norms come from? Second, I want to understand why particular individuals are responsive to and evaluable under particular social norms. Note that neither of these are causal questions; I am not going to provide a causal explanation of either phenomenon. Rather, I am interested in the basis for the normativity of social roles and the normativity of the demands placed on individuals by virtue of the social position they occupy. Giving a causal explanation of the normative contours of our social world is a worthy endeavor, but it is not my task here. Causal explanations address what we, in fact, do or will do, but they do not explain why we *ought* to do what we in fact do or will do, which is my topic here. But is there a question about social norms other than the causal question? Is there a distinctive form of social normativity? Is social normativity real?

## Is Social Normativity Real?

Thus far I have been assuming that social role normativity is a real category of normative obligation—that there is something here to explain or to understand. But it may seem reasonable to ask whether social normativity is a distinct (or real) category of normativity. Perhaps what a mother ought to do because she is a mother just follows from the special moral duty we have to family members? Maybe the ought of social norms is just an ethical ought? Or alternatively, perhaps social norms are merely prudential rules that allow us to avoid punishment or seem to offer the best payoff. Perhaps a mother figures out what she ought to do by considering which course of action will lead to better results or outcomes, for herself or for others, than the other possible courses of action. Maybe the ought of social norms is just a prudential ought?

In either case the suggestion is that social normativity is not a distinct type of normativity. Rather, social norms are either ethical norms applied to concrete situations, the applied ethics view, or social norms reflect a type of prudential thinking in a context, the prudential norm view. In either case social normativity turns out not to be a distinct type of genuine normativity. If the applied ethics view were true, then there would be no need to explain the source of normativity of social role norms, because it would be inherited from the ethical norms. If the prudential thinking view were right, then there also would be no normative oomph to be explained. End of my project!

One way to think about social norms, like those governing a mother's maternal activity, is as an application of moral principles governing familial relationships to a particular relationship in a particular culture. The idea is of a general rule and its application in a context. The normativity attaches to the moral principle itself, and only derivatively to the realization or instantiation of it. Strictly speaking the normativity in question is ethical, and while there may be lots of questions about the source of ethical norms, there are no special questions about the source of social norms because their normativity derives from the ethical normativity—wherever that comes from.

However, this way of thinking about social normativity is not adequate to the phenomena in several ways. First, not all social norms fit the applied ethics view because some social norms are prima facie not in accordance with, much less applications of, ethical principles. Social norms are often limiting, oppressive, and unjust; including some of the norms one ought to enact by virtue of one's social position. For example, one might think (as I do) that many gendered norms are like that. Indeed, many social contexts are unjust, and the injustice is often lodged at least partially in the governing social role norms. And so, it is hard to see how the normativity of social roles in general is to be explained by the ethical principles they realize in a social context. The important fact that many social role norms, which we ought to follow given our social positions, are unjust or oppressive needs to be accounted for in our explanation of the normativity of social role norms. But it is difficult to see how there could be a critique of a social norm that you ought to be responsive to, given your social position, if the normativity of the norm rested on nothing but an application of ethical principle. And another requirement facing our account is that it must explain people who are critical of the norms they stand under as well as those who are social role nonconformers. These are an important part of the phenomena of social role normativity.

A second way that social norms do not fit the applied ethics model is that social normativity includes normatively evaluable activities that do not fall within the range of standard ethical theories. Artisanal examples exemplify this point: around here there is a way the carpenter ought to make a corner, but this is not an ought-to that is an application of a purely ethical principle to a context. There is no ethics of corners! So, this is another way in which there is a poor fit between the range of phenomena covered by the concept of social normativity and the explanation of its normativity as applied ethics.

The idea that social normativity is applied ethics does not do a good job of accounting for the full range of phenomena that we would want it to cover. So, I suggest that we not think that the source of social role normativity derives from the moral principles that it exemplifies in concrete situations. And I suggest further that we look for another source of social role normativity. This is my project in this book. However, one might react to the case I have made against the applied ethics view of the source of social role normativity and conclude that social norms are really codified forms of prudential reasoning and lack any genuine normative oomph. If that were the case, then again there would be no need to try to explain the source of their normativity beyond a desire to avoid punishment or garner reward. There would be nothing more to explain.

Just as it is a mistake to think that social role normativity is best explained as the application of ethical norms to a concrete social context and that the normativity derives from the ethical norm, so too it is a mistake to think that social norms have merely prudential value. It is simply not the case that social role obligations track rewards and punishments. What I ought to do as a mother is not explicable in terms of seeking rewards and avoiding punishments—even though what I actually do might well be. What I ought to do as a mother can diverge from what might be best for me prudentially. It might be best for my child, and hence what I ought to do if I called in sick, even though calling in sick might lead to dismissal, lower pay, or a worse schedule. But if I acted prudentially, I would not be acting as I should, given that I am a mother. What I ought to do as an academic might diverge from my prudential best interests. I ought to evaluate students fairly, but in current circumstances it would be prudent for me to give very high grades to all students in my classes regardless of their performance. The prudential decision and what I ought to do as a teacher diverge. The source of normativity of social roles is not to be found in prudential reasoning or considerations.

Since neither the applied ethics view nor the prudential characterization of the source of normativity of social norms is persuasive, we have good reason to think that there is a genuine question to be addressed concerning the source of the normativity of social roles. Social role normativity is a real category of obligation with genuine normative oomph. But the source of social role normativity remains mysterious. How might we best explain it?

## The Artisanal Model

My account of social role normativity takes crafts, such as carpentry or cooking, and arts, such as flute-playing, as central exemplars of social roles. Social roles are teachable methods or ways of doing something in a manner that encodes social knowledge (*techniques*), and that involve the acquisition of powers or abilities to engage skillfully with the world by employing those techniques (*expertise*). The normativity is grounded in the function or work to be performed, well or badly, by employing the relevant expertise and techniques. As Aristotle says, "the good and the well is thought to reside in the function (*ergon*)" (*EN*, 1.7, 1097b26–27).[2] I introduce the term "Afunction" to label this constellation of ideas, which differs in important ways from functional attributions in the social and biological sciences.[3]

Rather than use examples of paths, borders, or money to set the stage for my inquiry into the normativity that characterizes social roles, I focus on the normatively rich, socially embedded range of

[2] Translations of Aristotle are based on Barnes.
[3] For an elaboration of this point, see Chapter 2.

techniques or expertise that comprise the arts and crafts. I think that the focus of social ontologists on paths, borders, or money is unfortunate, and leads in a misleading direction on the issue of social role normativity. If one wonders what makes a path, the right path, the one to be taken, then it seems that an individualist response in terms of human preferences or endorsement is the only available one. What could make a path the one to be taken if not the agreement and endorsement of an individual or a group of individuals? Dirt and grass are normatively impoverished. But if, instead, the paradigmatic cases of social roles are artisanal techniques, then there is a much richer set of resources to draw on in our understanding of their normativity. That a particular note is the note to be played, or a tool the very one for the job, is not simply a matter of an agent's preference or endorsement, or indeed the preference or endorsement of multiple individual agents. There is, in these cases, a technique that serves a function that grounds the normativity. Now, of course, that technique and function exist at all may depend on the existence of human cultures, but their existence does not depend on any proximate preference or endorsement by any individual or group of individuals in the vicinity. In fact, the direction of fit is the reverse: the technique and function that comprise the social role determine what is to be done, that is, what ought to be done by an individual who occupies that social position.

Adapting an idea from Aristotle, I argue that the source of social role normativity lies in the work or function performed by the social agent who occupies a given social position. Being an academic or being a mother is a social position whose occupants are responsive to and evaluable under a set of norms that taken together constitute a social role. Social roles are normatively assessable techniques of doing or making things that are embedded in and reflective of the way we do things around here. And I argue that we are responsive to and evaluable under a particular norm just because we occupy a social position that has that norm as part of the associated social role.

## Internalism and Externalism

It is useful to distinguish two general approaches to the question of the source of social role normativity: internalism and externalism.[4] I use the term "internalism" to refer to views that develop some version of the idea that both the source of social role normativity and the reason why particular norms attach to particular individuals originate in the same place, namely in the subject or agent herself. Some internalists root the normativity in the preferences of social agents either individually or as a group.[5] These are the Humeans. Others explain the normativity in terms of the autonomy or self-legislation of the norms by the agent. These are the Kantians. Hegelians elaborate on this Kantian theme by developing "a social recognitive form of the autonomy model" according to which "each individual is responsible only for what she has authorized others to hold her responsible for" (Brandom 76). What these views share is a

---

[4] Internalism and externalism are used to label opposing views in a wide range of philosophical topics from ethics, to semantics, to philosophy of mind. Here, I use them to label opposing views of the source of social role normativity. Social role normativity is a species of normativity and in what follows I use the term *normative externalism* to refer to externalism with regard to the source of social role normativity. I hope that my explanation of their use here will ward off possible confusion. See Chapter 2 for a detailed description of the distinction between internalism and externalism and my use of it. In earlier work, I used different terminology to describe an adjacent distinction. There I used the terms "voluntarism" and "ascriptivism" to label two opposing views on how it is that membership in a social kind is established. Voluntarism holds that membership in a social kind requires subscription by the individual, and ascriptivism holds that membership in a social kind is fixed by one's social position occupancy, the conditions for which are social, often determined by others, and context-specific. My focus in this book is on an adjacent issue that is downriver from the question of what establishes social kind membership; namely, how to explain the source of the normative oomph of social roles. There is an important distinction between the conditions for the occupancy of a social position, like being a carpenter or being a mother, the social role that someone occupying that position ought to perform, and the source of the normativity of that social role. The contrast between internalism and externalism demarcates two explanations of the source of social role normativity rather than the conditions for social kind membership. See Witt, *The Metaphysics of Gender*, 43–47.

[5] I find it useful to associate the different versions of internalism (and externalism) with figures from the history of philosophy, but I don't intend these associations to stand as interpretations of the philosophers in question. If the historical labels aren't useful to you, feel free to ignore them.

focus on the subject (or subjects)—her preferences, endorsements, or recognitive attitudes—as the source of normativity, including social role normativity. According to these views, social normativity enters the world through the attitudes of the persons who are subject to the norms. In addition, for internalists an agent is responsive to and evaluable under a social norm because she prefers it, self-legislates it, or authorizes others to hold her responsible for it. So, the internalist has a seamless and integrated explanation for both the origin of social role obligation and the reason why a given individual is responsive to and evaluable under a particular social norm.

I use the term "externalism" to refer to positions that root social role normativity in the social world itself, in its positions, institutions, and larger architecture. The core insight of externalism is that in some circumstances the structure of an enterprise or activity can bring with it normative demands quite independently of the attitudes of those who engage with it. Lawson's social positioning view sees the process of assigning a person to a social position as at the same time situating the person in relation to others by means of a package of rights and obligations. Other externalists point to games and model social normativity on the rules of a game that one ought to follow if one if playing the game. The idea of normativity as rule following does not depend directly on the attitudes of the players, but rather on the notion that in order to play the game one must follow the rules. Still others argue that social norms are elaborations of biological normativity. While these theories are externalist, they are not the version of externalism that I will develop here.

My version of normative externalism models social role normativity on artisanal normativity. Think about artisanal social roles, like being a carpenter or a baker, and the norms that shape and infuse the techniques that these artisans use, given the functions or the work that they accomplish. Artisanal normativity is not grounded in the artisan's preferences, endorsements, or recognitive attitudes; rather it is a matter of proficiency with a learnable technique or expertise. Being a carpenter and being a baker are social roles that are governed by techniques that realize functions and shape activities. Following the technique is what you ought to do, given that you are an artisan of a certain type around here, given that you occupy that social position. There is no additional subjective or internalist requirement to attach social role norms to an individual or to make them (collectively) something that individual ought to do.

Of course, it will often be the case that the carpenter prefers to use a level to square a corner, or a baker endorses weighing out ingredients rather than using cup measurements. Indeed, both carpenter and baker might understand themselves in relation to these identities, and so think that these techniques are to be done because of them. The point is that—for the externalist—these preferences or endorsements are not the factors that explain the normativity of the social role, nor are they the reason that an individual stands under an artisanal norm. Because if the carpenter does not prefer to use a level or a baker does not endorse use of a scale for measuring dry ingredients, they simply are not doing what they ought to do, employing the proper skill or expertise, insofar as they occupy these artisanal social positions. Their preferences or self-legislation do not determine what the right thing to do is; their preferences or self-legislation are not the source of normativity.

There is an understandable tendency to want to explain (or to explain away) social normativity, including social role normativity, in non-normative terms. It might seem strange and excessive that social norms track an irreducible kind of genuine obligation that is distinct from the normativity attaching to ethical principles. The idea adds a layer of normative complexity to the social world. This could be viewed as an entirely unnecessary epicycle or, alternatively, as providing a useful amplification that enriches our normative, ontological, and explanatory resources and vocabularies. In this book I make a case for the latter view.

The explanation of social role normativity on offer here is nonreductive. It does not attempt to explain the source of social role normativity in terms that are not normative. Rather, it takes artisanal norms as exemplifying social role normativity in general, and it attempts to generalize features of the artisanal model to other social roles. These features include the normatively infused notions of expertise and technique (*techne*) which will be explored in some detail. The notions of technique and expertise also point to the irreducibly social and interpersonal character of our social roles. The artisanal model illustrates the process by which we become skilled experts through habituation under the guidance of an expert who mastered the technique in question. What is passed on is not merely particular processes and practices, but also the standards and norms that are intrinsic to the craft. With the process of habituation comes both specific know-how and a general sense of excellence; what it is to do something well. Moreover, the apprentice also learns the reasons for the various techniques learned or what I will call "know-why." And this aspect of artisanal transmission lays the groundwork for norm criticism and social role nonconformity.

## What Is a Social Role?

Social roles demarcate ways of being human. Examples of social roles include being a carpenter or a baker, being a mother or a father, being a president or a professor, being a woman or being Asian American.[6] I begin by emphasizing that social roles are ways

[6] In "Role Obligations," Michael Hardimon focuses on the normative aspect of institutional roles, distinguishing between contractural roles (roles we sign on for) and noncontractural roles (roles we are born into). The latter he restricts to familial and civic roles, saying, "being a member of an ethnic group is not a role" (4). But the arguments Hardimon makes in relation to the legitimacy of obligations in relation to familial social roles also apply to ethnicities, races, and genders. In some contexts ethnicities are social roles and, like race and gender, are closely intertwined with familial roles. I agree with Hardimon's view that there are social role obligations that are noncontractural, but take the point further here by arguing that the source of social role normativity of both types

of being human rather than characterizing them primarily as a vehicle that establishes kinds of humans, because I want to highlight the idea that these roles normatively structure our social *activity*. So, even if Mallon is right that social roles are also "central mechanisms of category construction" and thereby directly relevant to the possibility of social scientific knowledge, my interest is in exploring their ontology, on what it is to be a social role rather than approaching social roles in relation to the possibility of social knowledge (*The Construction of Human Kinds* 58). If one views social roles primarily in relation to social kind construction, then one central issue will be how these kinds can achieve sufficient stability to be objects of social scientific knowledge in a fashion parallel to the way in which natural kinds are objects of scientific knowledge. This is, of course, an important question. But it is not the central question driving my inquiry. I am interested in social roles as normative ways of being human—of being in the social world—and in the puzzle of the source and nature of their normativity.[7]

Social roles are best viewed as techniques and expertise attached to social positions, and their normativity is grounded in the functions or work they enact. Being a carpenter is a social position that includes mastery of a technique that constitutes expertise (involving tools, materials, and others) that is evaluable in relation to the function of making things out of wood. Being a mother is also a way of being in the world that includes a set of expertise and techniques that are evaluable in relation to the activity

---

is noncontractural to use his terminology. Hardimon's distinction between contractural and noncontractural social role obligations blurs the distinctions I draw between the conditions for occupancy of a social position, the social role that someone occupying that position ought to perform and the source of the normativity of the social role.

[7] Amie Thomasson proposes a normative model of social groups according to which social group concepts function to normatively structure our lives together. Thomasson's focus on the normative structure of our lives together bears some resemblance to my project, although her emphasis on self-identification and group membership diverges both from the primacy I assign to social roles and my externalist orientation. Also, unlike Thomasson, my goal is to explain the source of social group or social role normativity. See "The Ontology of Social Groups".

of mothering. A bit more controversially, I propose that we think of gender and race along the same lines, as social roles, as ways of being human.

Viewing race and gender as social roles, as ways of being human, might seem to strain the resources of the artisanal model. The artisanal metaphor might not seem to be apt or a good fit for these examples. How well do the ideas of expertise and technique fit race and gender? In what sense does being gendered or being raced correlate to a function or to work? As I explain in Chapter 3, the artisanal model includes both arts that result in a product, like carpentry, and those that are realized in an activity, like playing the piano. Like being a mother, being a woman is realized in normatively evaluable activities or techniques rather than in relation to a product.[8] Also, the artisanal model seems to lack the ability to represent important aspects of these social roles. What resources does the artisanal model have to represent the hierarchical relations among genders and races? How well does it represent the oppressive relationships among genders and races? In Chapter 7 I explore the resources of the artisanal model to express relationships among social roles, including hierarchical and oppressive relationships.

The term "social role" itself is useful to consider, as it gestures in two directions that will be central for my argument. The idea of a *social* role underlines the notion that these ways of being a person are communal; whatever else a social role may be, it is a public, shared way of being. This feature counts against individualistic theories of social role normativity. For example, rational choice theory conceives of social norms as informal rules that govern social behavior where the normativity is grounded in either the rationality or self-understanding of individual social agents.[9] Some

---

[8] It is possible to interpret the maternal social role in terms of both activities and product, the child, in relation to which the activities are evaluated. However, it is not a part of maternal practice around here to consider a child to be a product.
[9] For a useful discussion of rational choice theory and social norms, see Bicchieri et al., "Social Norms."

rational choice theorists understand the rules as serving specific functions—like solving collective action co-ordination problems, enhancing social welfare, or holding us accountable to one another by enabling praise and blame. Rational choice explanations often characterize adherence to social norms (including social roles) in terms of a payoff maximizing strategy; in this case primarily one of avoiding sanctions. Here the rational self-interest is calculated for each individual separately. Alternatively, game theoretic accounts of social norms are interpersonal, and understand a norm as an equilibrium (e.g., a Nash equilibrium) of a strategic interaction. The latter approach emphasizes the role of mutual expectations in conforming to social norms, but it is the mutual expectations among rational, calculating individuals. My conception of social role normativity, in contrast, is not anchored by individual, intersubjective or group preferences about rules and rule-following. Individual preferences do not play a fundamental role in my explanation of social role normativity.[10] Rather than think of our social agency as elaborate poker games in which each player pursues their rational self-interest in a sequence of independent bids, we should think of it instead as comprised of sets of social techniques having multifaceted connections and rich normative content—as exemplified by artisanal and artistic skills and techniques.

The idea of a social role emphasizes the functional character of the normatively assessable activity. It connects the notion of an ergon –a function or work—to that of a norm infused human activity, or, in other words, a technique. A role is a way of being human; a set of normatively infused techniques that we engage with insofar as we occupy social positions that form part of the architecture of the social world (the culture that we inhabit). The notion of a role gestures toward both an activity and its normative dimension, and these are key elements in the phenomenon I address here.

---

[10] My project is to understand and explain the source of normativity of social norms, and it is unclear that rational choice theories focused on individual preferences have the same explanandum.

Each art or craft, each technique, is associated with a function or with a kind of work, and the normativity associated with the notion of a technique is grounded in the specific function or work that is performed. A skilled potter makes good pots, and a good ukulele player plays the ukulele well. My thesis is that social role normativity, in general, is explained by the function, the work or activity to be done, and the related techniques and expertise that constitute a given social role. The function is the work or activity, and the social role is comprised of various techniques and expertise that constitute ways of realizing the function. Collectively, social roles demarcate techniques of living, ways of being human or being a person. It is important to underline the fact that social roles are always local. They are our way of realizing a function; our technique for living; our way of doing things around here.

There are many instrumental norms intertwined in artisanal practices and other social roles, but there are also distinctive, noninstrumental norms that reflect local standards of excellence. Think about cooking norms, which seem to be primary candidates for an instrumental analysis—after all we need to eat. But now also consider the wide variety of cooking techniques that reflect the way we ought to do it—around here. In this context, there are normatively assessable practices and activities that constitute excellent cooking, and that excellence is not explicable in terms of instrumental values. Quite the contrary. The social world is packed with roles that have norms that cannot be given an instrumental justification. Maternal activity is again a good example—there are many ways or techniques of realizing maternal excellence in normatively assessable activities that have local standards of excellence that are not and could not be explained in purely instrumental terms.

## The Artisanal Model and Social Agency

An externalist theory of the source of social role normativity might seem to leave little room for the social subject, the agent, who occupies social positions, engages with various social roles, thinks critically, and creates a meaningful life. Where in my picture is there room for critical thinking, commitment, and creativity? The artisanal model can help in answering these questions. Notice that the very same questions could arise for artisans and artisanal activities, yet we do not find the fact that artisans are responsive to and evaluable under norms or techniques to imply that they are not also critical selves and creative selves. Similarly, I will argue that the various normative obligations that we undertake as we occupy social positions are both limiting and sources of freedom, power, and agency. Just as the expertise and technique of an artisan are both restrictive and enabling, so too the various norms we are responsive to and evaluable under enable important forms of social agency, including critique, creativity, and other ingredients of a meaningful human life.

Three challenges to the artisanal model are particularly important to itemize and to address in what follows. The first challenge is that the artisanal model apparently lacks resources to explain the rational criticism of social role norms by those who are responsive to and evaluable under them by virtue of their social position occupancy. But social role nonconformers and critics exist, and moreover, the fact that they exist is an important aspect of social role normativity. The second challenge is that the artisanal model lacks resources to explain normative creativity or normative self-creation, and normative self-creation is an important part of forging a meaningful life. Finally, the artisanal model seems to invite counter-examples—like the good thief and the expert enslaver. Certain social roles are inherently bad, like being a thief or being an enslaver, and it seems paradoxical to think of them on the artisanal model. What skills are involved? What notion of excellence? Are these *techne* really what one ought to do in any sense? How well does the artisanal model cope with examples like these? In more general terms, the third challenge asks what resources the artisanal model has for criticizing social roles that are embedded in unjust or oppressive hierarchies, like racialized or gendered social roles. To address this issue, we will need to consider how social roles are related to one another in the social fabric on the artisanal model.

## Coming Attractions: A Synopsis of *Social Goodness: The Ontology of Social Norms*

*Social Goodness* falls into two parts. In the Chapters 2–4 I introduce the artisanal model for social role norms. I begin in Chapter 2 by distinguishing two basic approaches to explaining social role normativity, which I call "internalism" and "externalism," and I make a case for externalism concerning the source of social role normativity. Then, in Chapter 3, I develop the artisanal model for social role normativity, borrowing the concepts of function, technique, and expertise from Aristotle. In Chapter 4, I describe the ontology underlying the artisanal model and explore its explanatory resources.

The second half of *Social Goodness* looks at several challenges facing the artisanal model. Chapter 5 explores the resources of the artisanal model to explain both the persistence and resistance to change of social roles, and our ability to criticize the norms that we stand under and to which we are responsive. The key idea here is that habituation—the transmission process of artisanal technique—is both normatively conservative and the source of our ability to be social role critics. In Chapter 6 I develop the resources of the artisanal model in relation to our ability to create ourselves, to be normative self-creators. I propose that the artisanal model provides a response to the paradox of self-creation, which asks how it is that we can create ourselves with new (to us) norms or values. How is that possible? If we do not already possess the norms, then how can we be guided by them? Alternatively, if we do already possess the norms, then there is no creation involved because we already endorse or are responsive to the norms in question. The artisanal model helps to unravel this paradox. Finally, Chapter 7 provides a glimpse of the big picture suggested by the artisanal model, and the holistic fashion in which social roles are normatively and ontologically intertwined in the social fabric. It explores the relationship between social role holism and the hierarchical and oppressive relations that often obtain among social roles.

# 2
# Social Role Normativity
## Internalism and Externalism

A professor ought to return graded work promptly; a carpenter ought to use a level. A central question facing any account of social role normativity is why the professor or the carpenter stand under these role-based norms. It is useful to distinguish the internalist response to this question from the externalist position. If you are an internalist about social role normativity, then you think that an agent is responsive to and evaluable under a set of norms because they prefer them or because they self-legislate them or because the norms have an intersubjective ground. The source of social role normativity for the internalist lies in the subject (or subjects), and in their attitude toward the norm in question rather than in their social position occupancy alone. In contrast, if you are an externalist about social role normativity then you think that an agent is responsive to and evaluable under the norms simply by virtue of their social position occupancy. If you are a professor, or a mother, or a carpenter, then certain norms apply to you, simply by virtue of your social position occupancy. Nothing further is required. In particular, the agent need not prefer the norm or endorse the norm, and it need not require intersubjective recognition.

I use the locution "responsive to and evaluable under a norm" to articulate the complex idea of social role normativity.[1] We act in and through our social positions (professor, mother, carpenter) which

[1] I do not intend to describe the full range of consequences of occupying a social position. In fact, occupying a social position often brings with it a broad range of entitlements and enablements. Because of my focus on social positions and social roles as sources of normativity, however, I will bracket many facets of social positions and roles that do not directly pertain to my topic. The phrase "responsive to and evaluable under a norm"

provide a normative perspective or standpoint for our agency. I distinguish between simply acting from a standpoint and acting from a standpoint that you prefer or have endorsed or self-legislated or with which you self-consciously identify. In acting from a standpoint or from a social position she occupies, an agent is responsive to a set of norms that are associated (in that culture and at that time) with that standpoint or social position. Responsiveness to a norm can range from full realization of it in activity to complete and total rejection. Most responses fall somewhere in between. Moreover, in occupying a particular social position the agent is evaluable (by others) under the norms that are associated with it. Of course, if the agent comes to identify with a standpoint or social position, then the associated norms can become explicit, and the agent might become a self-legislator of the norms. But being responsive to the norms or evaluable under them requires neither their self-legislation nor even explicit awareness of them.

It is important to distinguish three things that are sometimes conflated in thinking about social role normativity. One issue concerns the conditions for social kind membership or social position occupancy. By virtue of what criteria is an individual a carpenter or a mother? A second issue concerns what normative obligations an individual incurs by virtue of being a member of that kind or by virtue of occupying that position. Finally, the third issue concerns the source of the normativity of the norms that one is responsive to and evaluable under by virtue of being a member of a kind or occupying a social position. My focus in this book is on the second and third issues rather than the first.

Two further clarifications are useful at this point. First, we might wonder about whether being responsive to a norm and evaluable under it come apart in some instances. For example, Oedipus, who

---

is meant to capture the aspect of social roles that pertains to their central normative function.

unknowingly murdered his father, might be evaluable under the norm of filial piety by others, but he was not acting in response to that norm when he murdered the elderly man he met on the road. Less dramatically, when we travel to a foreign culture, we might well be evaluated under a norm that we are not responsive to because we are not aware of it, and it was not part of the repertoire of social norms we acquired growing up. Second, notice that there is a difference between the factual condition of being evaluated under a norm and the condition of being evaluable under it; the latter is the relevant condition for standing under a social norm.

Here is another way to describe the difference between internalism and externalism as explanations of the source of social role normativity. Consider gendered appearance norms, like wearing make-up or high heels for women in contemporary Western cultures. Now consider a gender nonconforming woman, by which I mean a woman who does not conform to her gender's norms of appearance. If you are an internalist about social role normativity, then the woman in question is not really gender nonconforming because she does not stand under the gendered appearance norms in the first place. Since she does not meet the internalist requirement of preference, endorsement, or intersubjective recognition, these gendered appearance norms have no grip on that person, and so she cannot be nonconforming with regard to them. For the externalist, in contrast, the woman is straightforwardly gender nonconforming insofar as she does not adhere to the conventional gendered norms of appearance in her culture, which she is responsive to and evaluable under by virtue of her social position occupancy. Nonconforming is a kind of response to a norm, but it presupposes that the norm is applicable to, and binding upon, the individual in the first place. As I will explain in more detail below, one of the strengths of externalism is that it makes social role nonconformity both possible and intelligible. Externalism underwrites the useful and important distinction between an individual being nonconforming and norms simply not applying to that individual at all. But, before considering the relative strengths of externalism and internalism any further, it will be useful to distinguish several forms of internalism and to explore each in turn.

## What Is Internalism?

I use the labels "internalism" and "externalism" for convenience to group together similar types of explanations of the source of social role normativity which might otherwise differ in many important respects. "Internalism" labels views that develop some version of the idea that both the source of social role normativity and the reason why particular norms attach to individuals originate in the same place, namely, in the subject or agent themselves. The latter issue is particularly pressing since all of us feel subject to social role normativity, but many of us might wonder *why* we are subject to it, especially in cases where the norms seem to be oppressive or at the very least a bad fit.

"Internalism" labels several different explanations of social role normativity, but each explanation locates the source of normativity in a "buy-in" or endorsement on the part of the social agent. Some internalists root the normativity in the preferences of social agents either individually or as a group. These are the Humeans. Others ground the normativity in the self-legislation of the norms by the agent. These are the Kantians. Hegelians expand on Kantian autonomy by adding the importance of recognition of and by others in establishing both normative obligation and in providing content for the norms. What all these types of internalism share is a focus on the subject and her commitment or pro-attitude as the source of social role normativity. Moreover, for internalists an individual agent is responsive to and evaluable under a social norm because she prefers it, she self-legislates it, or because the subject recognizes the authority of those responsible for the norm in question. So, the internalist has a seamless and integrated explanation for both the source of social role normativity and the reason why a given individual is responsive to and evaluable under a particular social norm.

Humeans think that agents are responsive to and evaluable under just those norms that the agent has reason to prefer. The central problem for these theorists is to account for the fact that some social norms are not in the agent's interest, and so, it becomes a question why the agent would rationally prefer to adhere to the norm. There are, of course, several possible responses to this problem, including Bicchieri's notion of a conditional preference: "People who have conditional social preferences care about what others who matter to them do and/or approve of. They have expectations that influence their behavior." (11)

The idea here is that our preferences include experientially generated expectations concerning what others will do and normative expectations of how others will react to what we do, and our preference to follow a social norm is conditioned on these expectations. This all makes sense. But notice that both the problem and the solution focus on how to explain why we have prosocial preferences and take for granted that social norm following is a matter of our preferences. The puzzle only arises if you ask—very reasonably—why we should prefer to follow norms that are not in our interest. And this question assumes that social role normativity is, at bottom, a matter of our rational preferences. Applied to social role normativity, the idea is that in addition to occupying a given social position the agent must also find the norms to be in accord with their conditional preferences. The Humean recipe for what makes an individual responsive to and legitimately evaluable under a social role is social position occupancy plus conditional preference.

Kantians are also concerned with the rational source of normativity. A powerful and persuasive version of Kantian internalism originates in the discussion of practical identity in Korsgaard:

Practical identity is a complex matter and for the average person there will be a jumble of such conceptions. You are a human being, a woman or a man, an adherent of a certain religion, a member of an ethnic group, someone's friend, and so on. And all of these identities give rise to reasons and obligations. Your reasons express your identity, your nature; your obligations spring from what that identity forbids. ("Personal Identity and the Unity of Agency" 83)

Korsgaard comments that obligations are often rooted in our identities, and she mentions social roles in particular: "A psychiatrist doesn't violate the confidences of her patient" ("Personal Identity and the Unity of Agency" 84). So, we have normative obligations rooted in our social position occupancies; so far, so good. However, that is not the whole story for a Kantian internalist like Korsgaard: "What we have established is this. The reflective structure of human consciousness requires that you identify yourself with some law or principle that will govern your choices. It requires you to be a law to yourself. And that is the source of normativity" ("Personal Identity and the Unity of Agency" 85).

The source of the normativity is not the social position occupancy (or pragmatic identity) itself, as it is for the externalist, but rather the internalist requires further that you identify with, or self-legislate, the law or principle governing your action. This is Kantian internalism. It differs from the Humean perspective, because it locates the source of normativity in the self-legislation of the agent rather than in the agent's rational preferences. For the Kantian, the recipe for what makes one responsive to and evaluable under a social role is social position occupancy plus self-legislation or endorsement of the norm in question.

Hegelians, in contrast, develop a social, recognitive version of Kantian autonomy.[2] The core of Kantian autonomy is retained in

---

[2] My description of the Hegelians is borrowed from Brandom, *Reason in Philosophy: Animating Ideas*, 52–108.

the notion that the subject is the only source of normative obligation. As Robert Brandom puts it, "I am only normatively bound when I have bound myself" (78). But the subject's commitment unfolds into the notion of reciprocal recognition: "Each individual is responsible only for what she has authorized others to hold her responsible for" (Brandom 76). Moreover, the content of the norm, what one is responsible for, is not determined or fixed by the subject but rather by those in the community who are recognized by that person to have authority. On the Hegelian story, it is not up to the individual to determine the normative content of the social roles she occupies; though that the norms in question bind her is a question of the subject's recognition of the authority of others in relation to her. Both the inclusion of recognition by others and the social determination of the content of social roles are elements that moves the Hegelian view into close proximity to externalism. However, so long as the only source of obligation is the self, even if it requires intersubjective recognition in addition, the Hegelian recognitivist keeps one foot firmly in the internalist camp.

According to my proposed taxonomy, Elizabeth Anderson's view might also count as internalism of the recognitive type. According to Anderson, "The normativity or 'oughtness' of social norms, then, is an 'ought' constitutive of commitments of collective agency. It is grounded in the perspective of collective agency, in 'our' shared view of how 'we' ought to behave. It is based on the fact that members accept the authority of 'us' to determine how each should behave in the domain defined by the norm" (193). The view of norms as normative attitudes (plus a knowledge condition) developed by Brennan et al. also could be placed in the recognitive camp at least with regard to the purpose of social norms, which is to hold one another accountable: "We must judge that one *must* do as the principles prescribe, or *expect* others to do so, or *disapprove* of those who don't, and so on. In doing so, we necessarily regard ourselves as accountable to others so far as complying with the principles is concerned" (38).

As we have seen, there are significant theoretical differences among the internalist positions we have just considered, even on the issue of the source of normativity. But they also share a core commitment to the idea that the origin of social role normativity lies in the attitudes of the subject herself, and not in the social world, and its web of positions, roles, practices, and associated structures. All internalists share the idea that the subject's acknowledgement of the force of the norm as obligatory in relation to themselves is that which constitutes its normativity. Strictly speaking, for the internalist there is no *social* role normativity because any normative obligation there might be in the world flows from the subject to the role and not vice versa. And it is just this shared commitment that makes internalism deeply implausible as an account of *social* role normativity. Whatever its merits might be as an account of some kinds of normativity, such as ethical or aesthetic normativity, internalism does not work well as an explanation of the source of social role normativity or an explanation for why an individual is responsive to and evaluable under a social role norm. And the reason for this is that with social role normativity both the origin of the normativity and its applicability to an individual is in some sense external to the agent and located in the social world. And internalism, in any of its forms, cannot capture and express this central feature of social role normativity.

## What Is Externalism?

As I use the term, "externalism" refers to positions that root social normativity in the social world itself: in its positions, roles, practices, and larger architecture. The core insight of externalism is that in some circumstances the structure of an enterprise or activity can bring with it normative demands quite independently of the attitudes of those who engage with it. Some externalists point to games and the way in which the rules of a game constitute it and provide a clear sense of normativity as rule following that does not depend on the attitudes of the player, but rather on the rule-governed structure of the game. You ought to move a bishop diagonally because you are playing chess. You might, in addition, prefer or endorse the move, but that it is what you ought to do does not require or depend upon your preference or endorsement. Perhaps social role normativity is like the normativity of rules in a game?[3] Or perhaps social role normativity is best captured by Lawson's social positioning theory that sees the process of assigning a person to a social position as at the same time situating the person in relation to others by means of a package of rights and obligations. Alternatively, an externalist might turn to the biological world and try to root social role normativity in our biology or our biological heritage. Perhaps it is the specifically human biological heritage as social primates, who occupy differentiated roles, that is relevant to the source of social role normativity.[4]

Another possibility, and the one I pursue in Chapter 3, is to think about artisanal social roles, like being a carpenter or a baker, and the norms that shape and infuse the techniques that these artisans should use, given the functions or the work that they accomplish. Perhaps artisanal social roles are paradigmatic of social roles quite generally. Artisanal normativity does not originate in the artisan's preferences, endorsements, or intersubjective recognition; rather it is a matter of correct technique and acquired expertise. Being a carpenter and being a baker are social roles that are governed by techniques that realize functions and shape activities. Following the technique is what you ought to do given that you are an artisan of a certain type, given that you occupy that social position. Moreover, the norms of correct technique are indexed to a specific

---

[3] For an excellent discussion of the rules approach to social normativity, see Joseph Rouse's description and criticism of normative regularism in "Practice Theory."
[4] See Okrent, *Nature and Normativity*.

social context, and not merely instrumental. This is shown by the variability of correct techniques in different societies and contexts even when the product or goal is the same. Think about variation in cooking techniques in different cultures as an example of both the context dependence of technique and its noninstrumental value. Of course, for humans, that food be effectively and efficiently cooked is instrumentally valuable; the point is that this does not exhaust the norms that characterize local cooking techniques.

A carpenter should use a level because of the kind of activity she is engaged with and the technique that she employs in her actions toward realizing her function. There is no additional internalist requirement needed to attach social role norms to an individual or to make them (collectively) something that individual ought to do. Although it might be up to an agent who is a carpenter that she tries to make things out of wood, it is not primarily up to the agent *how* she should go about making those things. Given the natural properties of wood, it can be used in making things only if a certain limited range of activities is engaged in. Given the impossibility of individuals discovering those methods on their own, only by following an historically and socially developed set of techniques will it be possible for those individuals to make anything at all. Of course, it will often be the case that the carpenter prefers to use a level to square a corner, or a baker endorses weighing out ingredients rather than using cup measurements; indeed, though perhaps less plausibly, both carpenter and baker might understand themselves as intersubjectively bound by these norms. The point is that—for the externalist—these attitudes are not the factor that explains the normativity of the social role, nor are they the reason that a particular role attaches to a particular individual. The direction of normative flow is the reverse; because the carpenter and the baker occupy the social positions that they do, certain norms pertain to them and govern their activities, and so they (often) will prefer or endorse them. Many of these norms concern the techniques of their crafts; and that these are the right techniques is grounded in the functions they accomplish and the work they do, and not in any attitude of the artisan toward them.

## The Case for Normative Externalism

Contemporary thinking about social normativity is overwhelmingly internalist; so much so that internalism is often simply presupposed without argument. To counter the prevailing attitude, I begin my discussion with several considerations that favor an externalist view of social role normativity. What can I say in favor of an externalist explanation of our entanglement in a normative web of social roles? Why accept the externalist explanation of why it is that an individual is responsive to and evaluable under a social norm? After all, the internalist story has a certain appeal in requiring that my assent or endorsement be engaged in order that a norm be obligatory for me. And what about morally or politically repugnant social roles? Surely, the occupants of some social positions should not stand under the associated norms? These look like compelling points in favor of internalism, and I will return to them below. But for now, I want to sketch out several considerations that favor externalism.

The first consideration is an appeal to examples of social roles where we are not inclined to cancel their normative force just because the person does not prefer or endorse the norm in question. I am thinking here of examples like maternal and paternal responsibility.[5] In the case of these social roles, it is clear that we would hold the individual responsible even if they would not prefer or endorse the norms in question. In the case of these social roles,

---

[5] For a relevant discussion of how social roles ground reasons, see Reid Blackman on deadbeat dads: http://peasoup.us/2017/01/roles-ground-reasons-internalism-false-reid-blackman/.

an individual is responsive to and evaluable under the associated norms just by virtue of being a mother or a father. The externalist explanation seems right.

Other social roles follow this pattern as well. Consider being a professor or being the president. In these cases, we hold individuals responsible to the relevant norms just because they occupy a certain social position. Or consider the obligation that a medical researcher has to disclose her ties to drug companies in her published research. Isn't this an obligation that the researcher has because of her social position as an academic and scientist? If the researcher does not endorse the norm (because she thinks the research is very important and would not be funded otherwise, or because she is confident that she is not prey to greed or undue financial influence) we do not think that she is no longer governed by the norm. This line of thought is intended to make externalism initially plausible by appealing to examples where it seems to provide the appropriate explanation for the phenomenon but internalism does not. We would want our explanation of social role normativity to cover these kinds of everyday examples.

I mentioned the second argument earlier. This is the idea that internalism lacks the conceptual space to accommodate the common phenomenon of a person rejecting or modifying a social role that they stand under, that is, as a social role nonconformer. It might be helpful to draw an analogy here with the philosophical discussion of functions. In the case of functions, it is important to be able to distinguish between the case where something, say a heart, malfunctions and the case where the entity simply does not have that function. When a heart malfunctions, it does not do what it is supposed to do. This is very different from some other organ, say the eye, not circulating the blood in a body. In the latter case the organ is not malfunctioning; it simply doesn't have that function. An adequate account of biological functions should underwrite a distinction between an item malfunctioning and lacking the function entirely.

Similarly, an adequate account of social role normativity should be able to distinguish the case where the social norm simply does not apply to the individual at all, and the case where the individual rejects, modifies, or fails to fulfill the norm they stand under. The latter cases require that the person is responsive to and evaluable under the norm in the first place. But for the internalist, if the individual does not prefer or self-legislate the social role norms, then that individual does not stand under the norm in the first place. The social role is not obligatory for, or even relevant to, that person.

Perhaps I underestimate the resources of an internalist perspective to maintain the difference between social role non-conformity and social role irrelevance? Recently, Katherine Jenkins has developed a norm-relevancy account of gender identity:

> On my account, which I will describe as the "norm-relevancy account," to say that someone has a female gender identity is to say that she experiences the norms that are associated with women in her social context as relevant to her. (728)

The idea that a social role attaches to an individual because of the individual's experience of the norms as relevant gives this account an internalist flavor and orientation. And Jenkins explicitly includes gender nonconforming attitudes and behavior under the umbrella of the norm relevancy account of gender identity: "Crucially, I understand 'experiencing a norm to be relevant to oneself' to be perfectly compatible with behaving in contravention of that norm and with disapproving of that norm" (730). Hence, Jenkins apparently offers an internalist account of social role nonconformity. The person experiences a norm as relevant to them, but either does not endorse the norm or does not act according to it. But is "experiencing a norm to be relevant to oneself" enough to establish that the individual stands under the norm in question for the internalist? It seems not. Experiencing a norm as relevant to oneself is just the experience of finding oneself responsive to the norm, which is quite different from affirming or having a pro-attitude toward it. The internalist requires some kind of preference or endorsement of the norm in question, which is more than, or other than, merely experiencing the norm as relevant. So, it turns out that the norm relevancy view does not provide an internalist account of social role nonconformity, whatever its merits as an account of gender identity.[6] Internalist accounts of social role normativity lack the conceptual resources to accommodate social role nonconformity.

Another consideration that favors externalism concerns how to understand and explain the normative conflict that is caused by the inconsistent normative demands of one's social roles. In Chapter 1 I remarked that as a mother I ought to put my children first, but as an academic I should value knowledge above all. These social roles can easily come into conflict in the real world. The externalist can point to the two social position occupancies as the source of the obligation to the two roles that generate the normative conflict and, more important, can explain the conflict's persistence even after a decision in a particular situation has been made. For the internalist, however, the persistence of the normative conflict is somewhat mysterious. Once you prefer or endorse the norms of one social role over the other, the conflict should dissipate. But this often does not happen; often the conflict persists. In order to have a genuine normative conflict, an individual must stand under both sets of incompatible norms, and the externalist story about this situation is better than the internalist story.

---

[6] It is important to note that Jenkins's primary focus is to develop an ameliorative account of gender identity and not a theory of social role normativity.

## The Case for Normative Internalism

Now let's look at a few considerations that seem to favor internalism. First, there seems to be something right about the idea that for a norm to be a norm *for me* that my preference or endorsement must be engaged. How can I be obligated by a norm that I do not even endorse? Second, internalism is an appealing position in that it pictures us as free self-creators of our values rather than as passive robots caught in the normative grip of various preprogrammed social roles. Third, internalism appears to provide an attractive account of the moral repugnance of certain social roles; these are roles that no one ought to prefer, endorse, or engage via intersubjective recognition.

To the first point, the externalist can concede that very often it is the case that our intentional commitments line up with what our social roles demand. But this coincidence of intention and obligation does not and could not establish the truth of internalism because we also observe occasions when preference and obligation come apart from one another. Recall the research scientist who does not prefer to disclose or who does not self-legislate disclosure. Indeed, even if preference and obligation always coincided, that would not establish the truth of internalism. Rather than revealing an internalist requirement for social role obligations, I think this intuition reflects the fact of regular coincidence between what we think we should do and what we ought to do, a connection that is formed by habituation into our various social roles. I have more to say about the role played by habituation in developing expertise in Chapter 5.

In response to the second point, the externalist can use the examples of the artisan and the artist to argue that the position not only allows for free and creative activity but is in fact a precondition for it. It is the skillful artisan rather than the raw beginner who is able to creatively change the techniques of their craft. Technique and skill are enabling factors that create power and ability rather than hobbling individual agency. The correct example of a skillful artisan is someone like the cellist Yo-Yo Ma whose technique and expertise are enabling and freeing rather than limiting and restricting. I elaborate on the artisanal model and its resources for what I call "creative selves" in Chapter 6.

The third apparent advantage of internalism might be the most important. Consider the repugnant roles of being an enslaver or a torturer; surely these are roles that no one ought to be responsive to and evaluable under. They ought not exist. How can externalism address the existence of morally repugnant social roles, roles that no one should be responsive to or evaluable under? Externalists are committed to the idea that if you occupy a social position you are responsive to and evaluable under the corresponding social role. The social position occupier is ipso facto obligated according to externalism. This seems deeply problematic. In contrast, the voluntarist can quarantine morally repugnant social roles by arguing that no one should prefer or endorse them. But notice that this argument, whatever precise form it takes, requires resources that transcend internalism as a theory of social norm obligation by appealing to arguments about what roles one *ought* to prefer or endorse and not what roles one is responsive to and evaluable under by virtue of one's endorsement.

So, it is not internalism as an explanation of the source of social role normativity that is doing the work here, but other arguments. Think about how an internalist would need to argue against the existence of a repugnant social role. Remember that internalism is simply a general orientation concerning the source of social role normativity. There is nothing about the internalist view in any of its forms that amounts to or provides resources to argue against the moral acceptability of a social role. Internalism tells us where the normativity comes from, its source, but it does not tell us where it is directed or where it should be directed. Additional resources, like ethical or political principles, are required to argue that a particular social role, or cluster of social roles, should not exist.

And, of course, externalists can also appeal to resources beyond its explanation of the source of social role normativity to criticize the existence of morally repugnant social positions. People should not occupy these positions and should not stand under these norms. There is nothing to stop an externalist from arguing that no just social structure should include a morally and politically repugnant social role, like being an enslaver. On this point, the two kinds of explanations of social role normativity are on a par; both require additional resources—beyond their explanations of social role obligation—to criticize the existence of morally repugnant social roles.

At this point, I have made a prima facie case for an externalist approach to social role normativity. I did so by considering points that favor externalism, by responding to possible criticisms of it, and, finally, by addressing apparent strengths of internalism. Despite its widespread unpopularity in contemporary philosophy, on balance there are good reasons to be an externalist about social role normativity. However, it might have occurred to the reader that the dichotomy itself is an oversimplification of the normative contours of our social world.

## Complications

I have been treating internalism and externalism as exclusive alternatives—as if either one or the other provides the correct explanation of the source of social role normativity. But the reader might think that the normative situation is more complex and nuanced than that. Perhaps both sources of normativity are required? Indeed, this is not an abstract possibility since the Hegelian recognitivist view that I placed in the internalist camp might more accurately be described as a kind of normative dualism. For the Hegelian, the obligation to the norm is intersubjective; it originates in the subject's authorizing others to hold them responsible, but the content of the norm, what one is responsible for, is not determined or fixed by the subject but rather by those in the community who are recognized by that person to have authority. The latter aspect captures the intuition that social normativity is importantly interpersonal and social rather than simply subjective or individual. In short, the recognitivist view offers an attractive picture of social normativity that integrates the autonomy of normative obligation with the intersubjective and social determination of normative content.

However, on the narrow but crucial question of the source of normativity or the origin of obligation, the recognitivist position falls squarely into the internalist camp. We are obligated to those norms that we recognize the authority of others to hold us accountable to. It is an enrichment of the Kantian self-legislation option because it incorporates intersubjective recognition, and the social determination of the content of the norms or what we are obligated to recognize. But the source of normativity remains the subject and for this reason it is an internalist theory of social role norm obligation.

A second possibility to consider is that the source of normativity for some social roles might be our preferences, self-legislation, or intersubjective recognition, while the source for others might be the social position occupancy itself, including the context of practices and structures in which the position is embedded. For example, we might think that it is the act of undertaking a marriage vow and our endorsement of the promises in the vow that is the source of their normativity. Imagine that we take the vow on a deserted island. We bind ourselves to the norms which are associated with the social role of being a spouse. Surely, the internalist story makes more sense with an example like this one. Other institutional social roles like being a professor or a president lend themselves more readily to an externalist interpretation of the source of their normativity. Perhaps social role normativity is a patchwork of different sources of normativity; some internalist, some externalist, and some a recognitivist blend. Even though externalism might explain the normativity of some social roles, the normativity of others is better explained by some version of internalism.

However, I actually don't think that the example of marriage vows on a desert island is a clear and uncontroversial example of a social role whose normativity has an internalist explanation. That one is married may depend upon the speech act of promising (in a particular social and historical context), but what one should do and that one should do those things depends upon the fact that you thereby occupy the spousal role, however you got into it. It is important to distinguish between three things; first, the conditions that determine our social position occupancy; second, the obligations follow from that social position occupancy; third, the source of those obligations. In the marriage example, we occupy the social position spouse by virtue of a particular speech act, an avowal. But it is because we occupy the social position of spouse that we are responsive to and evaluable under a set of norms. And, according to externalism, the source of the normativity, the source of the normative oomph, is the social position occupancy—that you are a spouse.

Even if we were able to cleverly craft another example with more potential for internalism, it would not make any difference to the import of the issue under debate between internalists and externalists. Because, for the internalist, the *only* source of normativity or obligation is the individual person. Externalism is a narrower claim, namely that *some* genuine normativity originates in the practices and structures of the social world. And, my claim here is that *social role* normativity is best explained by externalism, by which I mean that for the most part we are responsive to and evaluable under social roles simply because of our social position occupancies. And it follows from this that there is normativity embedded in the structure of the social world, and that internalism as a general theory of social normativity is false.

But, if one doesn't explain social normativity as originating in the preferences, self-legislation, or intersubjective recognition of the social agent, then—literally—where does it come from? In Chapter 1 I criticized the project of trying to explain why a path in the woods was the path to be taken as a way of approaching social normativity including social role normativity. I pointed out that dirt and grass were normatively impoverished and that this example (and others like it) seems to require an internalist explanation. Where else would the normativity originate? It is one thing to criticize the starting point, presuppositions, and shortcomings of internalism and quite another to provide an alternative externalist explanation of the source of social role norms.

In Chapter 3 I develop an externalist explanation of social role normativity. This view of social role normativity sees social roles as ways of being human that are best exemplified by artisanal roles, such as being a carpenter or being a cook. These artisanal activities exemplify an externalist approach in that preferences, endorsements, and intersubjective recognition are not the source of artisanal norms—the norms that are reflected in the notions of technique and expertise. Rather than thinking about paths, borders, or money, or reflecting on tools and artifacts, I take being an artisan as a paradigmatic social role and explain social role normativity (in general) in terms of the expertise, techniques, and functions associated with being an artisan, a cluster of concepts that together I call "Afunctions" (short for Aristotle functions).[7] As we will see, taking artisanal social roles as paradigmatic allows us to incorporate the material, historical, and institutional embeddedness of social roles in our account, and to center the importance of social context and local norms.

Finally, although there are many instrumental norms woven into artisanal practices and processes, these do not exhaust their normative profile. Artisans are responsive to and evaluable under

---

[7] I use the neologism "Afunction" (short for Aristotle function) to distinguish the Aristotelian framework of artisan, technique, expertise, and function from discussions of functions in other areas of philosophy. See Chapter 3 for more on this point.

norms of excellence that are internal to their craft and that cannot be understood in purely instrumental terms. This point is suggested by the wide variation in craft standards of excellence in different cultures and times and by the fact that some of these standards do not have immediate or even distant instrumental value. In broader terms, the artisanal model of social roles norms precludes a complete explanation of the normative oomph of social roles in terms of the instrumental value of solving a social coordination problem or enhancing social cooperation. I develop this point further in Chapter 7.

# 3
# The Artisanal Model

"The excellence of each thing is relative to its proper function."

Aristotle, *EN*, VI.1, 1139a16–17

There are many dimensions to the topic of social normativity and many approaches one could take. This book focuses on social role normativity, which is the normativity that attaches to social positions like being a mother or father, being a president or a professor, being a carpenter or a flute-player, or being a woman or an Asian-American. One reason for my focus is that all human societies include social positions and associated roles in their ontologies, while differing in the particular social positions and roles available. So, if we could understand the normativity of social roles, we would understand something central to the normative structure of our social environment.

## What Is Social Role Normativity?

Consider former U.S. president Donald Trump. His decisions, statements, and actions were criticized from many perspectives and for many reasons. For example, some of his actions on January 6, 2021, might have been illegal or might have been unethical in that they might have compromised his oath of office. However, in addition to the legal or the ethical criticisms, a central line of criticism focused on his social position and the idea that some of his actions or statements were unpresidential. They were not responsive to the norms associated with being president, with occupying that social position. Yes, it is wrong to use crude language about one's opponent, but it is particularly wrong for a president. Yes, it is wrong to bend the truth, but it is particularly wrong for a president. Yes, it is wrong to exploit one's profession financially, but it is particularly wrong for a president. You get the idea. Even though its exact content is debatable, there is a social role, a set of norms that attached to Trump because he was president, not because he endorsed them or promised to keep them, but because he occupied that very social position. Notice that Trump's behavior as president was not predictable in relation to the cluster of norms that make up the presidential role: the social role can fix what the occupant ought to do, but it cannot always and reliably predict what an individual will do.

Being a president, like being a priest or being a soldier, is a social position of which some of the duties are voluntarily, publicly, and explicitly undertaken by the individual in question. For example, Trump's obligation to protect and defend the U.S. Constitution was publicly and explicitly undertaken in his oath of office. However, the social role of president extends far beyond the rather narrow terms of the oath of office, as we can see in the wide array of criticisms of Trump as unpresidential. It was unpresidential of Trump to mock a handicapped reporter; it was unpresidential of him to flout public health advice and rules; it was unpresidential of him to decline to participate in the Biden inaugural.

Social positions, like being president, are locations in the structure of the social world that are lodged in its practices and institutions. It is important to distinguish cleanly between the social position and the social position occupier; between the status of being a mother and the individual who is a mother, the individual who occupies that position. Indeed, unlike being a U.S. president, many positions, like being an academic or a mother, can be occupied by multiple individuals at a time, as well as many more individuals over time. Social positions structure the social fabric. Moreover, social position occupancy brings an individual under the umbrella of a social role, which is comprised of one or more social norms to which the individual is responsive and under which the individual is evaluable by others because of their social position occupancy.

While the existence of social positions and roles in human societies is obvious, the source and the character of their normativity is not. In Chapter 2, I developed the distinction between internalism and externalism, which provides a useful frame for introducing this topic. Recall that an internalist thinks that an individual is responsive to and evaluable under a social norm because she prefers or self-legislates the norm, or because the norm has an intersubjective ground. For the internalist the fact that an individual occupies a given social position might make her a candidate for responsiveness and evaluation, but normative obligation requires, in addition, that she prefers, endorses, or identifies with the norm. In contrast, an externalist thinks that a norm attaches to an individual just because she occupies a social position where that norm is part of the social role associated with the position. I argued that for many social roles, externalism is true, and the norms apply to individuals simply by virtue of their social position occupancy. For the externalist, a mother or a father is responsive to and evaluable under maternal and paternal social norms (which of course vary from society to society) simply because the individual is a mother or father.

Externalism is a general perspective on the source of social role normativity, but it is not itself a theory or explanation of the source of the normativity attached to the social position. It is still necessary to develop a plausible externalist explanation of social role normativity, that is, to develop an account of the origin or source of social role normativity that does not root it in the attitudes of individual subjects. In this chapter I do just that. I propose a theory or a model for understanding the source of social role normativity: the artisanal model. This is my answer to Anderson's puzzle and question with which I began this book: "The great puzzle of social norms is not why people obey them, even when it is not in their self-interest to do so. It is, how do shared standards of conduct ever acquire their normativity to begin with?" (191).[1]

It is a puzzle how the norms associated with a social role could exert normative authority in relation to an individual. After all, social roles vary from society to society and are embedded in different constellations of practices and different kinds of social structures. And while we can tell a descriptive or anthropological story about the social norms in a society or in human societies in general, such a story does not establish or require that the norms in question are irreducibly normative (collectively), and also (individually) open to assessment as legitimate or illegitimate. These two requirements on our theory of social roles—that they are irreducibly normative and yet open to critical assessment—might seem to pull in opposite directions, but I take it that an adequate explanation of the source of social role normativity should do justice to both requirements. In this chapter, I address the first requirement and postpone the issue of normative critique and assessment to Chapter 5.

## The Artisanal Model

My suggestion is that the source of social role normativity is an individual's social position occupancy. It nails the social role to the social position occupancy itself rather than appealing to the agent's attitudes toward those norms. My proposal brackets the question of the basis for social position occupancy; it is neutral on the question of what explains our various social position occupancies or,

---

[1] It is worth noting here again that this is not Anderson's response to her question. For Anderson the source of obligation is our self-understanding as a member of a group, as a family member, for example.

in other terms, the grounds for belonging to various social kinds. Rather, it is a view downstream of these issues, and it concerns the normative consequences of, or what is entailed by, an individual occupying a particular social position however that is determined. But where does the normativity reside in the externalist picture? Following Aristotle, it is useful to think about social roles as constituted by a function or by work that is to be realized in an activity or in actions:

> For just as for a flute-player, a sculptor, or any artist, and, in general for all things that have a function or an activity, the good and the well is thought to reside in the function, so would it seem to be for a human being, if he has a function. Have the carpenter, then, and the tanner certain functions and activities, and a human being none—is he naturally functionless? (*EN*, 1.7, 1097b25–30)

This is, of course, Aristotle's famous function argument. I am not interested here in exploring the argument itself in any depth.[2] In particular, I am not concerned to examine Aristotle's inference from the existence of artisanal functions to the existence of a human function. Rather, I want to focus on certain ideas about artisans, functions, and norms, and the relationships among them, that the argument presupposes. From this constellation of ideas in Aristotle I distill the notion of an Afunction. I will use the term to refer to several interrelated ideas concerning artisanal functions and activities that I extract from Aristotle's texts, explain in this chapter, and use to explain the source of social role normativity. Particularly important are the core ideas of technique and expertise that together describe artisanal agents and their activities. The concept of an Afunction is a central component of the artisanal model.

---

[2] For an insightful interpretation of Aristotle's function argument to which I am indebted, see Barney, "Aristotle's Argument for a Human Function."

A little background and context for our text will be useful. In the preceding chapters Aristotle has been pursuing a normative question concerning what the final—that is, most complete, self-sufficient—good is for a human being. Aristotle thinks that by identifying the final good he will be able to fill in some content to the notion of *eudaimonia* or human flourishing, which all agree is the end or goal of human life. His strategy here is to argue from the existence of a function (and a good) for a human being occupying a social position, to the existence of a function (and a good) for a human being simpliciter. Rachel Barney notes, "The builder and the shoemaker *are* human beings, identified *qua* practitioners of a certain craft [*techne*]; they are socially constructed *kinds* of human beings, or *roles* or *identities* that a human being may take on" (297).

Now for Aristotle (and for Plato) crafts, like building and making shoes, and arts, like flute playing, are intrinsically normative activities; each activity realizes a function that is associated with an excellence in relation to which the function is performed. So, for Aristotle, function or work is a normative concept tied to the excellence of a thing and its good, and not merely a descriptive term attaching to a person's job or occupation.

Artisanal functions or work, like carpentry, are comprised of activities that are normatively assessable; they can be performed well or badly. There are good and bad carpenters because some carpenters display a high degree of expertise or skill and others do not. Artisanal functions in this respect are unlike mathematical functions or causal role functions that are not intrinsically normative. Moreover, the normativity of artisanal functions or activities is not purely instrumental.[3] The standard of excellence for being a

---

[3] Brennan et al., in *Explaining Norms*, deploy a distinction drawn by March and Olsen between a "logic of consequences" and a "logic of appropriateness" to describe the noninstrumental character of social role norms (157). Appropriate behavior is assessable in relation to a given social role in a particular social context, and not simply in terms of the consequences of following (or not following) the norm. Given your social role, this is the norm you should follow.

good carpenter, for being skilled and having expertise, is not simply a matter of instrumental goods like delivering a good quality product. In addition, there are aspects of skill and expertise that are local, the way we do things around here, and cannot be cashed out in instrumental terms. Indeed, some local standards of excellence might lack instrumental value entirely.

My suggestion is that if we think about the source of social role normativity in relation to Afunctions using the artisanal model, then the normativity of the social role flows from, and is grounded in, a normatively infused notion of function, work, or activity. Aristotle points to the conceptual connection between function or work (*ergon*) and activity (*energeia*) in the *Metaphysics* (*Met.*, 8, 1050a21–3). To be a carpenter is to perform a set of actions and activities that are normatively assessable in relation to the function or work of being a carpenter, of being what one is. But to be a mother is also to perform a set of actions and activities that are normatively assessable in relation to the work of being a mother, of being what one is. And so on for other social roles. Recall that it is important to distinguish between the conditions for the occupancy of a social position, like the conditions for being a carpenter or being a mother, and the norms that constitute the social role that someone occupying that position ought to be responsive to. A person can become a mother by giving birth to a baby or through adoption, but once a mother, the person is responsive to and evaluable under maternal norms.

Aristotle and Plato differ both in their central examples of functions and in their understanding of functions, and these differences are important for my purposes.[4] For Plato, a tool is the paradigmatic case of a functional being, and a tool requires both a designer and a user to have and to realize its function. The function of a tool is extrinsic in that both the origin and the realization

---

[4] See Barney, "Human Function," for a discussion of the differences between Plato and Aristotle on function.

of the function refer to entities external to the tool itself. For this reason, the normativity of a tool can be given an external, instrumental explanation. A hammer is to be used to drive nails; it was created with, and is used by, a carpenter for that purpose. Tools are paradigm instances of functional entities with instrumental value.[5]

In contrast, Aristotle's central examples in the function argument (and elsewhere) are *artisans* not artifacts. Both the source and the realization of the function or work obtain just insofar as that individual is an artisan of a certain kind. A function and identity go hand in hand. "This relation to end and identity makes *ergon* a powerful normative concept closely linked to the good of a thing and determining what counts as its excellence or virtue (*arête*)" (Barney 301). For a person to be an excellent flute player is to function well qua flute player, and neither the source nor the activation of the function is external to the flautist. Artisans, unlike tools, are not paradigm examples of functional entities with instrumental value; instead, their norms are rooted in their identity and the standards of excellence that define the relevant function or activity. Taking artisanal agency as paradigmatic allows us to develop a noninstrumental, contextual interpretation of social role normativity. What counts as a good carpenter or flautist is indexed—in a profound way—to the society in which the activity occurs, and it is this deep contextuality that underwrites that some of the goods in question are noninstrumental.

Some social roles, like being a flautist, are primarily comprised of actions, like practicing and performing and, in these cases, it is the actions alone that are measured in determining excellence. Indeed, Aristotle famously distinguishes between action (*praxis*) and production (*poiesis*)—between activities like flute-playing that have no product beyond the activity itself, and arts like house

---

[5] In fact, Aristotle's view of artifacts like tools is complex. He recognizes both intrinsic ends of artifacts, the functions that they ought to realize, and their extrinsic ends or uses. See Witt, "In Defense of the Craft Analogy."

building, which are activities that can be done well or badly, but also have a product that is an independent standard by which to judge both the agent (the builder) and the activity (the building). As Sarah Broadie puts it, "The craftsman's good productive activity, is in one sense, his end: the perfection of him as a craftsman. The product, which is other than the activity, is his end in a different sense: it is that by which one judges his success, hence judges him to have achieved his end in the first sense. We assess the excellence of the making, hence of the maker, by the quality of what is made" (207). In the case of actions, the evaluations are indexed to the actions themselves, but in the case of production there is an external standard as well—the product. Although the normativity in the case of production (*poiesis*) is more complex than in the case of action (*praxis*), in both instances the value is noninstrumental in the sense that they are realizations of the craftsman's end or function, of what it is to be an artisan of this kind. Insofar as the individual is an artisan they realize their functions, their excellence as an artisan, in their artistic or productive activities. This excellence or goodness, this expertise, is intrinsic to being an artisan, to what the artisan is, and not merely instrumental as in the function of a tool.

Taking artisanal normativity as paradigmatic of social role normativity is useful as illustrating the way in which social roles are embedded in material and social worlds. Being a flute player is an intrinsically *social* role that requires both the recognition of others (teachers, fellow orchestra members, audiences) and a rich social context including a learned and shared technique. Being a flautist is also a *material* role in that there are many material conditions that surround the social role: the instruments, the buildings, the sheet music. And, of course, instruments, buildings, and sheet music themselves are situated in a complex web of material, historical, and social conditions. Artisanal roles exemplify the complex situatedness of social roles in general. For further discussion of the situatedness of social roles, see Chapter 7.

Of course, my emphasis on the material and cultural context leads to the thought that what makes someone a good flute player in Brussels today might differ from what made someone a good flute player in Aristotle's Athens in the sense that both the techniques for playing well and the aesthetic properties that constitute playing well might differ, and so the abilities and expertise of a good flautist might differ as well. But this is entirely consistent with there being objective criteria and norms of excellence for what counts as playing well and being a good flautist in each context. It is not up to the individual flautist to decide how to play well or what counts as playing well around here. In this regard being a flautist is like being a mother or being a president, in that the activities and attitudes that constitute being a good mother or being a good president might vary among different societies. Nonetheless—and even in cases where they are deeply contested within a culture—there is an underlying presupposition that there are shared and objective local norms for being a good mother or a good president or good flautist around here.

The complex and deep social embeddedness of artisanal social roles and activities goes hand in hand with the idea that the standards of excellence are local. Even though there are different Afunctional norms at different places and times, there must nonetheless be some such norms at all those places and times. There might be different norms for being a good carpenter at different places or times, but there are no places or times where human carpentry can occur without there being some norms for being a good carpenter rooted in the work to be performed by carpentry. In sum, the Afunction view of the normativity of social roles provides a model for local, socially embedded, noninstrumental standards of excellence.

It is important to be clear that in proposing that we use the notion of an Afunction to explain social role normativity, I am not using the notion of function either as it appears in the technical discussions of functions in the philosophy of science and the philosophy of biology, or the way it is used in the social sciences. I return to this point later in this chapter. Rather, I use a more commonplace idea of function or work, exemplified by arts and crafts, that we find presupposed by arguments in Aristotle and Plato that are intelligible to us—even if they are not ultimately persuasive.[6] Note also the *Oxford English Dictionary*'s definition of "function" as "the special kind of activity proper to anything. The mode of activity by which it fulfils its purpose."

In light of the OED definition, it is important to clarify that an Afunction is not a purpose understood as an intentional goal. When Aristotle says that the good resides in the function, or in the action, he might be taken to be referring to the intention or purpose of the flautist; for example, the intention to play well that day. And, indeed, playing beautifully might be the goal of the performer that day. But this is not what Aristotle means when he says that the good resides in the function or work. Rather, he means that the activity itself, as an expression of the flute-playing function and technique, is also an expression of the virtue or goodness of the artisan qua flute player. Flute playing consists of normatively evaluable techniques. And that it is so is a fact independent of the intention of the musician, although often the intention to play well, and the activity of playing well will line up. But, for Aristotle, the player's intention is not the source of the normativity of the activity; that is intrinsic to the activity itself and grounded in the function of flute playing and its standards of excellence.

At this point it is worth considering two influential and important interpretations of Aristotle on these topics, those of Korsgaard and MacIntyre, to underline common themes and to identify important differences from my view. Korsgaard, whom we already encountered as an internalist on the source of social role normativity, has developed a series of insightful and sympathetic

---

[6] *Republic* Book 1 352e–354a contains another example of an argument that presupposes a folk notion of function exemplified by arts and crafts.

interpretations of functions in Aristotle and Plato, including a detailed interpretation of Aristotle's function argument ("Aristotle's Function Argument" 129–150). I have used Aristotle's function argument to inspire the artisanal model for social role normativity, which is an externalist view on the source of social role normativity. But I have also described Korsgaard as a paradigmatic internalist on the source of social role normativity. So, it would be useful at this point to clarify briefly where our interpretations of the function argument overlap, and where they differ.

Let's begin with one important point of agreement, which is how to understand the Aristotelian notion of function. Korsgaard distinguishes a function from a purpose (what a thing does) and suggests rather than an Aristotelian function is "how a thing does what it does" (138). This idea, that function refers to the way a thing does what it does, corresponds to the notion of technique as I use it in the artisanal model. And, for Korsgaard, the way a human being does what it does is through reason and rational activity: "rational activity is how we human beings do what we do, and in particular, how we lead our specific form of life" (141). Artisans exemplify the ways that individual humans do what they do, namely, by engaging in rational activity. For example, an architect "must understand not merely that the bricks and timbers are arranged thus and so; and that the house must withstand the winter storms; but how this very arrangement of bricks and timbers enables the house to withstand the winter storms" (139).[7] The architect's know-how corresponds to the notion of expertise in the artisanal model.

The identification of rational activity as the way in which we humans do what we do is undoubtedly one conclusion that could be drawn from the function argument. And it is a conclusion that Aristotle builds upon in subsequent books of the *Nicomachean*

---

[7] Later I describe artisanal expertise as comprising both know-how and know-why and the latter captures Korsgaard's idea that the architect knows how the arrangement of bricks allows the house to withstand the winds.

*Ethics*, which ends with an argument that the best human life is one of contemplation or pure rational activity. Korsgaard's emphasis on rational activity as the characteristic human way of doing things also blends smoothly with her internalist perspective about the source of normativity, given the additional assumption that the rational activity at issue in artisanal activity is correctly pictured as a form of self-legislation. It is this assumption that I take issue with.

I think the artisanal examples in Aristotle's function argument can be read in another way to suggest an additional facet of the way we do what we do, and an alternative way of characterizing artisanal rational activity. Often, we do what we do using techniques, which are shared and normatively assessable ways of doing and making things. It is by virtue of being an architect, by virtue of occupying that social position that a person is responsive to and evaluable under local architectural norms, and so it is occupying the social position of architect that explains why you are responsive to just these norms in this situation; for example, why one kind of roof is better than another in the circumstances and given local norms and resources. In relation to the social and shared normative dimension of *techne*, artisans like architects can serve as models for how externalist social normativity works. This externalist interpretation of the artisanal examples in Aristotle's function argument is compatible with a focus on rational activity as the way we do things; it simply specifies further that the rational activity in question is not individual self-legislation, agent by agent, but rather it is shared and social. It is acting in a manner responsive to and evaluable under shared norms or techniques which are the ways in which we do things around here given the social positions we occupy.

With his idea of a practice, Alasdair MacIntyre also captures something of the Aristotelian and commonsense notion of a function realized in activities guided by expertise or technique: "By a practice I am going to mean any coherent and complex form of socially established cooperative human activity, through which goods internal to that form of activity are realized in the course of trying to achieve those standards of excellence which are appropriate to, and partially constitutive of, that form of activity..." (187).

MacIntyre lists arts, sciences, games, and politics as examples of practices. The important point, for my purposes, is that with the idea of a practice MacIntyre singles out a kind of social activity that has an internal normativity or, in other words, goods or norms to be realized that are noninstrumental. Further, because MacIntyre's practices are defined as cooperative human activities, they presuppose cooperation, and so their normativity could not be fully derived from their value as instruments of social coordination, on pain of circularity. Of course, practices might also have instrumental value because of their contribution to a stabile social organization or as solutions to coordination problems; but this instrumental value does not exhaust the normativity of practices. For a further discussion of social positions, social roles, and social coordination see Chapter 7.

Unlike MacIntyre, my focus is on the agents who are embedded in his practices, and not the practices themselves. Nonetheless, MacIntyre's idea of social practices is useful in describing a normatively rich social context within which agents occupy social positions with roles that are expressed in activities characterized by noninstrumental normativity. The agents manifest the standards of excellence that are "appropriate to and partially constitutive of that form of activity." MacIntyre's standards of excellence are what I refer to as the expertise and techniques associated with social roles.

MacIntyre's discussion of practices is useful in the picture it paints of our social world as rich with shared human practices that have local standards of excellence. It is also worth pointing out that the norms in this social world are not depicted as originating in the preference, self-legislation, or intersubjective ground of rational subjects, but rather in the standards of excellence that are constitutive of the activities and practices themselves. In other words, MacIntyre's practices are fully compatible with, and indeed an attractive expansion of, the externalist approach to social role normativity that I endorse.

For Aristotle, the expertise and techniques characteristic of the activities of artisans and artists, the standard or norms by which they are evaluable, are both acquired powers in individuals (expertise), and bodies of shared and teachable social knowledge (techniques). They thread the needle between subjective and objective, between individual and social world. Expertise is not merely a subjective disposition existing in an individual; it encodes a shared social knowledge, which is not up to the individual to determine. There is no private expertise. And, although techniques are shared and teachable social knowledge, they are also practical and embodied because they are realized in and by the activities of artisans pursuing their crafts. Techniques are not abstract Platonic forms of artistry and craftsmanship; they are normatively assessable ways of doing and making things that are realized in the skillful actions of artisans and artists.

## Functions in Social and Biological Contexts

It may be useful at this point to distinguish the concept of an Afunction that I use to explain social role normativity from structural functionalism as a concept in the social sciences and from the philosophical discussion of functional attributions in the case of biological and artifactual entities. Structural functionalism, as I understand it, is a view of society as a stabile arrangement of parts that function together to achieve harmony, or some other social good. And the normativity of a functional part is instrumental and derives from the end or goal to be achieved or the larger whole to which the part contributes. This is not the idea that I borrow from Aristotle. First, as I mentioned above, the Afunction's possible contribution to a larger social good—the Afunction's instrumental value—cannot be used to explain the normative oomph of local standards or expertise that makes one a good practitioner around here. This is both because inefficient and unpopular norms persist, and because they often emerge for reasons that have nothing to do with instrumental value. The local standards or norms to which an artisan is responsive may, in fact, not contribute to larger goals like social cooperation and stability. The two sources of value come apart in some cases. To call someone "an excellent cook" refers to local standards pertaining to the activity and product of cooking—tastes good, nutritious, economical—rather than to the instrumental value that the activity of cooking might have as it contributes to a larger societal good like the economy. Think about how the expertise displayed in cooking a filet mignon well diverges radically from the catastrophic impact of beef production and consumption on the environment and on social stability.

There is a large philosophical literature on biological functions and on what we mean when we use functional language generally. Two views of functions are particularly prominent. Millikan has developed the idea of a proper or etiological function of a feature, in terms of the self-replicating features of an organism. Alternatively, Cummins has developed a theory of systems functions, in which the function of something is identified relative to a system; in principle things can have more than one function (741–764). I am interested in a different question from both Millikan and Cummins, which is how to explain the normativity that attaches to social roles that individuals are responsive to and evaluable under. I use an ordinary language, "folk" notion of function, as did Aristotle and Plato, in developing the notion of an Afunction.

There is also an extensive philosophical literature on the normativity of biological and artifactual functions.[8] In the philosophy of biology, the central issue is how to understand the normativity of

---

[8] For example, see the articles in Krohs and Kroes, editors, *Functions in Biological and Artificial Worlds*.

the parts of organisms like the heart. What does it mean to say that the heart has a function, something it ought to do? Note that the heart's function is neither what it actually does (some hearts malfunction) nor what it could do (in fact, some hearts could never circulate blood) but rather what it is to do or ought to do (circulate blood). A similar issue arises for artifacts, which also seem to have functional normativity that is difficult to explain in causal terms. An artificial heart has the function of circulating blood; that is what it ought to do, not simply what it can do or is doing. While the question of the source of normativity addressed here with regard to organisms and artifacts is similar to my question concerning social role normativity, the range and nature of the entities clearly differs. Just as there are important and relevant differences between organisms and artifacts, so too, social roles differ from both of them in significant ways. One key difference concerns the fact that social roles are ways of being human; they are ways of enacting our social agency. So social role normativity raises a host of issues concerning what it is for an agent to respond to a norm and what it is for an agent to be evaluated by others under a norm that I group together under the dichotomy of internalism and externalism. Corresponding to the complexity attaching to social role normativity is a rich set of resources to explain or to ground that normativity (the notions of expertise and technique), and these resources are not directly relevant to either organisms or artifacts and hence are not immediately available to ground or explain their functional normativity.

We can use the metaphor of the watch, its parts, and the watchmaker to contrast the normativity of biological and artifactual functions with the normativity of artisans and artisanal activities. The parts of a watch have functions in relation to the function of the whole, which is timekeeping. If the parts are functioning properly the watch keeps time, and the parts are doing what they *ought* to do. The watchmaker, in contrast, is engaged in a series of activities that are normatively assessable not only in terms of whether they result in a functioning watch but how well they do so, and if they do so in accord with local norms, values, and standards of excellence.

## Social Role Norms as Rules of the Game

A plausible alternative way of explaining social role normativity (that is compatible with an externalist perspective) is to think that social norms are like the rules of a game. Playing a game like chess requires a player to follow the rules; a rule specifies what a player ought to do—if she is playing chess. The rules specify which moves are legal, what one ought to do in this situation with that piece, and which moves are not legal. Those are moves one ought not to do. Similarly, the demands of a social role could be explained by conceiving of the role as a game with rules that ought to be followed given that one occupies a particular social position. A president ought to follow the rules that specify what a president ought to do; a mother ought to follow the rules that specify what a mother ought to do.

Of course, the rules of chess just specify the legal moves of the game; the moves that one can make and the moves that one cannot make. But one can play legal chess without playing either competent chess or expert chess. There are strategies or heuristics for playing chess that presuppose the legal rules and that constitute expertise in playing the game. For example, don't sacrifice a piece of greater value for a lesser piece. But notice that it is being responsive to the rules that specifies what an individual ought to do given they are playing chess (and not checkers). The strategies and heuristics that an experienced player employs are evidence of additional skill or expertise. But skill and expertise are elements in the artisanal model of social normativity, and so the amplified interpretation of the rules-of-the-game explanation for the source of social role normativity would no longer stand as an explanation entirely independent of the artisanal model. I assume in what follows that the rules-of-the-game explanation of social role normativity refers rather narrowly to explicit or implicit rules, and not to the various kinds of strategic amplification that constitutes skill in chess and other games.[9]

The rules of a game provide a clear sense of normativity as rule following that does not derive directly from the attitudes of the player or players, but rather from the rule-governed structure of the game itself. The rightness or wrongness of various moves is not determined by the attitudes of the players. Adopting Rouse's terminology, for the regulist, both individuals and practices gain normative traction by considering them to be rule governed, like games, where the rules specify both what players ought to do and what moves count as appropriate.[10] Maybe the normativity of social roles should be explained using the model of rule-governed games?

I respond to this suggestion in two ways. First, I present several criticisms of regulism as an account of social role normativity. Second, I point to certain features of the artisanal model that makes it a better, richer resource to explain the source of social role normativity than the rules-of-the-game alternative. None of these considerations taken in isolation provide a conclusive argument against the rules-of-the-game understanding of the source of social role normativity or an argument in favor of the artisanal model. However, I do think we can conclude from this discussion that the artisanal model is richer and more plausible than the rules-of-the-game explanation of the source of social role normativity.

One well-known criticism of regulism stems from a regress argument concerning rules made by Wittgenstein. The regress argument has a broad target, namely any rule-governed activity, and

---

[9] Thanks to Bill DeVries for suggesting this amplification on what might be meant by the rules of the game of chess.

[10] For more discussion of the rule conception of normativity, I recommend Joseph Rouse's description and criticism of normative regulism in "Normativity." Rouse also canvases several other approaches to providing a ground for social norms.

hence is not directed precisely against viewing rules as explaining social norms. However, it does apply to the rules-of-the-game thesis. Here it is. Begin with the idea that no rule interprets itself and how to apply it. Hence, to apply a rule correctly would seem to require another rule that specifies how to do that. And so on. Let's apply this to the rules-of-the-game explanation of social normativity. In order for the rules-of-the-game explanation to work, there must be some way of distinguishing between breaking a rule and just playing another game. Or playing the same game but just using a different interpretation of the rule. But to make these distinctions one needs a rule for the correct application of a rule, and so we generate a regress. Note again that the regress argument has a broad scope and applies to any rule-governed process including, but not limited to, playing games.

A second criticism concerns the *kind* of explanation regulism gives for social normativity. The rules approach can only establish a kind of descriptive regularity because rules-of-the-game normativity originates in the acceptance by the community of the standards or rules in question. To see this point, consider again the regulist's central example of games. Ultimately, the rules of a game have normative authority only to the extent that, and dependent upon, their acceptance by the players. The regulist explanation is not able to explain the externalist "ought to do–ness" of social roles because it lacks explanatory resources beyond the social acceptance of a group of individuals. There is a gap between the fact of social acceptance and normative authority, and the latter does not follow directly from the former. The fact of social acceptance can account for an informal rule being normal in the sense that it demarcates what most people do or accept; but the fact that most people follow a certain convention does not render it something that they ought to do.

Neither of these criticisms applies to the Afunction explanation of social role normativity. While some social roles might include formal and informal rules, the explanation of their normativity is not based on rule following, and so Wittgenstein's regress argument concerning rules is not directly relevant. Also, the Afunction explanation of social normativity does not establish a merely descriptive normativity based on social acceptance. The normativity arising from the notions of function, technique, and expertise is not simply a matter of social acceptance but rather is grounded in the requirements for excellence intrinsic to an activity. That a cook should weigh out ingredients or a carpenter use a level does not rest upon widespread social acceptance of these practices, but rather it reflects a kind of artisanal normativity that attaches to the role via the notions of technique, expertise, and function. It is what you ought to do or ought to use given that you occupy a certain social position, when that is understood to imply a technique and an expertise. So, neither of these lines of criticisms of the rules-of-the-game explanation of social role normativity applies to the Afunction explanation.

Finally, a rules-of-the-game approach to social role normativity is unable to sustain criticism of the individual norms that constitute social roles. Rawls argues that it is a point of logic that you can't criticize the rules that constitute a practice, but only the whole practice itself (3-32). The reason for this is that if the rule (partially) constitutes the practice, then without it (the rule) you wouldn't have that very practice. This point makes sense if we are taking games like chess as paradigmatic examples of rule-governed practices. It makes no sense to criticize the rules of chess, because without following the rules that constitute chess you wouldn't be playing chess. But the same "logical" point does not hold concerning the criticism of whole practices, like criticism of the game of chess. The game of chess can be criticized from any number of perspectives. Perhaps it is a waste of time. Or perhaps it is a sexist or a classist activity. So, on the rules' conception of the source of social role normativity, it is just not possible to engage in internal criticism of individual norms but only criticism of social roles. And this is a serious drawback of the rules view of the source of social normativity.

Like the rules-of-the-game approach, the artisanal model of the source of social role normativity allows for criticism of whole social roles or practices. But it also allows for internal criticism and innovation of the individual norms that an individual is responsive to and evaluable under insofar as they occupy a particular social position. This is a clear advantage of the artisanal model, since individual social role norms are often criticized, and our account of the source of social role normativity ought to allow for this type of criticism. It is part of the phenomena to be explained. I have more to say about the critical resources of the artisanal model in Chapter 5.

There is much more that could be said about each of these criticisms and none of them singly is decisive. Ultimately, however, it is the rich explanatory resources of the artisanal model of social role normativity that make it clearly superior to the rules-of-the-game account. Let me spell out a few of the most important features:

1. Afunction normativity is fully context-sensitive: What one ought to do, how one ought to do it, when one ought to do it, and so on, depends entirely on context. The rules of the game lack this context sensitivity. When playing chess, the rook always moves in a rectilinear fashion and ought to be moved that way no matter who one is playing or where, or on what kind of board, and with what kind of pieces.
2. Afunction normativity is flexible: Artisanal flexibility, which comes with expertise, is a good model for the ways in which social role norms can be adaptable and flexible. Rule following tends to be an on-off switch and most games do not provide a good model for the complex context of the social world in which the flexible expression of social role normativity is the rule and not the exception.
3. Afunction normativity captures the normative variety characteristic of social role normativity. For example, norms of beauty, appearance, and utility are interwoven with other norms in artisanal activities, like cooking or carpentry. And

we find them interwoven in other examples of social role normativity as well. Consider gendered appearance norms or the complex of values (including gendered appearance norms) that attach to being a professor. Rules and rule following lack this normative richness and center on an abstract notion of correctness.

4. Afunctions are interconnected with one another and with other types of social structures and practices in a way that captures the way in which social roles are interconnected with each other and with multiple features of the social world.

5. Afunctions are intertwined with the material world and provide a model for understanding how norms are embodied in other social structures and subject to material conditions.

Although an externalist might explain the source of social role normativity in terms of rule following and might think of social norms as (informal) rules, this explanatory framework provides an impoverished set of resources that fails to capture the full complexity of what social role normativity is. In particular, the rules-of-the-game interpretation does not articulate the flexibility, richness, context dependence, and materiality of social role normativity and the many ways in which it is related to other threads in the social fabric. We have good reason to favor the artisanal model over the rules-of-the-game model in our externalist explanation of the source of social role normativity.

We also have good reason to prefer the artisanal model to Lawson's social positioning theory. Lawson's social positioning theory is a general theory of the constitution of social life, which it depicts as processural and relational. Social positioning is an ongoing process (processural) and it always places persons and things in relation to other persons and things (relational). As Lawson puts it, "Processes of social positioning are in operation 'everywhere that human interaction occurs, no matter how simple or complex the forms, or how harmonious or conflictual the setting'" (18).

However, Lawson's social positioning theory is not simply an ontology of the social world, an accounting of its basic furniture. It is simultaneously an explanation of the source of social normativity, and in particular the source of social role normativity. According to Lawson, when social positioning occurs and when a person occupies a social position, they are both oriented toward a function *and* enmeshed in a package of rights and obligations in relation to others. Lawson's social positioning ontology is functional, relational, and normative.

Lawson's social positioning theory is an alternative (and plausible) externalist explanation of social role normativity. Lawson's picture of the source of social normativity is externalist because the normativity of the packet of rights and obligations originates in the social positioning rather than the attitudes of the persons positioned or the position itself. In this respect Lawson's social positioning ontology resembles the artisanal model that also grounds social norm obligation in social position occupancy. It is also similar because it focuses on the idea of a function or work to be done in characterizing what social positions are like. In addition, like the artisanal model, which envisions a network of interrelated social positions and social roles, Lawson's packet of rights and duties relates persons through their normative commitments to one another, which are engaged through social positioning.

The chief difference between the social positioning view of social constitution and the artisanal model concerns the way in which the normative component is characterized. Lawson's rights and duties are essentially interpersonal normative relationships. To use an example of Lawson's, in the café the waiter has the duty of serving the customer; the customer has the right to be served. Artisanal norms include interpersonal rights and duties; for example, the chef has a duty to pay the line cook, and the line cook is responsible to the chef for various tasks. But artisanal norms are not limited to interpersonal rights and duties. Other artisanal norms, like a baker's weighing ingredients rather than measuring them, are world and material involving, are responsive to technique, and are not directly interpersonal. To return to Lawson's example, while it is true that someone socially positioned as a waiter thereby has a duty to serve the customers, arguably that person is also responsive to and evaluable under other norms that together constitute expertise for a waiter, such as being (or appearing) attentive to the table and respectful to the customer. So, one difference between the two theories is in the complexity and "thickness" of social role norms that each can capture and express. As an explanation of the source of social role normativity, the artisanal model has a richer normative vocabulary than Lawson's social positioning theory. Occupying social positions like being a mother or being a president entails a broad array of normative obligations, only some of which are captured by the idea of rights and obligations. Since the artisanal model can provide an externalist picture of social role normativity that includes rights and obligations but also includes other kinds of norms, it is a richer model and a more complete model of social role normativity.

Moreover, the artisanal model does a better job of capturing the material and cultural situatedness of social norms than does the social positioning theory. The artisanal model is world involving as well as interpersonal. The artisanal model captures and expresses the normativity that characterizes social positioning that has material conditions and works on social reality in a material way. Artisanal technique, what ought to be done, is always deeply contextual and dependent on material conditions. The artisanal model can depict the many facets of situatedness of social norms. Lawson's social positioning theory does include the social positioning of objects (tables, chairs, implements) as well as persons, but even with this addition, Lawson's theory doesn't fully incorporate the situatedness of social norms. Social positioning theory is a relational view between persons and objects but does not articulate or incorporate the full material situatedness and locality of social role norms. It pictures a web of normative relations among the occupants of social positions but does not tether that web firmly to the material world.

Finally, Lawson's theory conceives of social positions as functional parts of larger networks or systems, but there is no theoretical explanation of their functional character. In other words, Lawson's normative packet of rights and obligations envisions the normativity of social norms as a set of relations among persons grounded by the process of social positioning. But this interpersonal, relational conception of normativity is different from the normativity grounded in the notion of a function or work to be done. And we might wonder how Lawson's theory accounts for the source of that aspect of social normativity. In contrast the artisanal model centers the notion of a function, or of work to be done, and can incorporate the interpersonal relational aspect within that framework. It is unclear how the relational web of rights and duties established through social positioning could also ground the functional normativity of social positions. For these reasons the artisanal model for social role normativity is preferable to Lawson's social positioning theory.

Although the artisanal model provides the most plausible externalist picture of the source of social role normativity, it does so by using notions such as expertise, technique, social position, and social role. And these concepts raise important and interesting questions about the underlying ontology of the artisanal model. The artisanal model seems to require ontological and explanatory resources that extend beyond ontological and explanatory individualism, which is the view that the social world consists of individuals and their attitudes and actions. What are the ontological underpinnings of the artisanal model? What explanatory resources does the model require?

# 4
# Social Norms and Social Reality

The picture of social role normativity sketched thus far has three basic conceptual components. Externalism locates the source of social role normativity in social positions and in associated social roles. These are independent of individual persons, their attitudes, and their actions. This is normative externalism. The artisanal model adds to normative externalism that the social positions are functionally defined, that techniques attaching to those positions are ways of performing social roles, and that expertise is the ability of an individual to employ appropriate techniques, responding to the appropriate norms, in a context. Given the sketch of social role normativity that has been developed to this point, we might wonder what picture of social reality or what social ontology is implied by externalism and by the artisanal model of social role normativity. In this chapter, I argue that normative externalism and the artisanal model requires a more complex social ontology and richer explanatory resources than is afforded by methodological individualism. It is important to note two caveats. The chapter provides an articulation of the outlines of the social ontology implicit in the artisanal model of social role normativity rather than an argument that that social ontology should be adopted. Nor do I offer a full ontology of the artisanal model of social role normativity, which would require discussion of the ontology of social positions, the nature of artisanal powers, and other important topics that lie beyond the scope of this chapter.

## Ontology, Explanation, and Social Norms

One way to frame questions about social ontology is in relation to the topic of methodological individualism. As described by Haslanger, methodological individualism holds "that the social world is made up of individuals, and so explanation of social phenomena should be in terms of the behavior and attitudes of individuals" ("Failures of Methodological Individualism" 1).

Methodological individualism combines commitment to an ontology of individuals, their attitudes, and actions, with explanatory individualism, the idea that explanations of social phenomena should be formulated in terms of individual persons, their attitudes, and actions. Ontological individualists think that individual persons and their attitudes or actions are ontological bedrock. As Ásta puts it, "The creators and maintainers of our institutions and practices are individual human agents" (127–128). Other social ontologists find individualism impoverished both ontologically and as an approach to explanations of social phenomena.[1]

It might seem obvious that normative externalism and the artisanal model are nonindividualist, both with regard to ontology and with regard to the explanation of social phenomena. And it is true that the explanations offered by externalism and the artisanal model, and the underlying ontology, are not limited to individuals, their attitudes, and actions. In that sense they are nonindividualist. However, it is important to notice that "individualism" and "nonindividualism" typically label rival types of causal explanations of phenomena in the social world.[2] Externalism, in contrast, is a theory about the source of social role normativity, and the artisanal model explains why it is that a particular individual stands under

---

[1] See, for example, Epstein, *The Ant Trap: Rebuilding the Foundations of the Social Sciences*.
[2] There are exceptions. For a project that explains social norms and the source of social normativity from the perspective of methodological individualism, see Brennan et al., page 17.

a particular social norm. These are not causal explanations of phenomena in the social world but rather noncausal explanations of important normative features of the social world. The individual is not caused by the social role to do anything in particular; responsiveness to a norm is not a causal relationship. Normative externalism and the artisanal model address different questions—about the source of social norms and the reasons that individuals stand under them. Being a mother, occupying that social role, explains why a person stands under a set of maternal norms concerning what that person ought and ought not do. But being a mother, occupying the social role, doesn't cause the person to do or to refrain from any particular action. Rather, being a mother, occupying that social role, explains something perhaps even more important, namely, why they *ought* to do certain things and *ought to* refrain from others.

Both the explanation I offer of the source of social role normativity and the explanation I offer for why individuals are responsive to and evaluable under social norms exceed the explanatory resources of individualism. Social positions, social roles, techniques, and expertise (the explanatory resources of normative externalism and the artisanal model) are none of them identical to, or reducible to, individuals, their attitudes, and actions. The individualist ontology is too meager to contain the resources necessary to formulate explanations of social role normativity that are externalist and understood in terms of the artisanal model.

To help clarify what the social position occupancy of an individual explains, let's consider an example. Both mothers and fathers ought to care for their children, according to the norms prevalent around here. But they ought to do so in different ways and with different priorities. That fathers and mothers occupy these different positions, with different roles attached, explains both why they are in general responsive to each set of norms and why they are evaluable under and responsive to different norms. Occupying those positions with those roles doesn't *cause* any particular action of the occupants. But it does explain their normative obligations and why they are different for differently gendered parents. And remembering Anderson, mothers and fathers are responsive to these (different) norms because they think they ought to be. And, to consider another example, when someone comes up with a better way to build a house, a better technique, this doesn't *cause* any particular action of any agent, but it might explain why it is that carpenters in the future in general conform to different norms and techniques.

Of course, at this point, it is open to the proponent of methodological individualism to reject normative externalism and to advocate internalism, which locates the source of social role normativity in individuals, in their rational preferences, self-legislation, or intersubjective recognition. To do this, the methodological individualist would need to address the arguments in Chapter 2 that favored normative externalism. There is no need to rehearse the arguments and considerations again here, however, because even if the arguments in favor of normative externalism prevail, the individualist has another perhaps more convincing gambit, which is to argue for reductionism concerning the conceptual ingredients of the artisanal model. If the elements that make up the artisanal model are all reducible to individuals, their attitudes, and actions, then the artisanal model is fully compatible with methodological individualism.

An individualist might respond to the conceptual ingredients of the artisanal model by arguing that both social positions and social roles are themselves explicable in terms of, and reducible to, individuals and their attitudes and actions. An individual who occupies a social position, like being an academic or being a mother, is an academic or a mother. To be an academic or to be a mother is simply to belong to a human kind. And human kinds are nothing over and above their members. Also, social roles, normatively assessable ways of performing functions, are enacted by the individuals who occupy various social positions—by individual mothers or individual academics. In this way the notions of social position and social role can be understood and explained without reference to anything other than individuals, their attitudes, and their actions. So, a methodological individualist might argue that, ultimately, the artisanal model does not require any explanatory or ontological resources beyond individuals, their attitudes, and their actions.

To assess this individualist proposal, we need to take a closer look at what a social role is according to the artisanal model. A social role is a normatively evaluable way of realizing a function or work. A social role is not equivalent to the attitudes or actions of any individual or any group of individuals because of its normative aspect. To say that a person (or a group of persons) has a pro-attitude toward doing a particular activity in a particular way does not explain why that individual *ought* to do it and *ought* to do it that way, though the pro-attitude might be part of a causal explanation of why they did it that way. Conversely, to say an individual (or many individuals) has a negative attitude toward performing a particular activity in a particular way does not explain why they *ought* not do it, or *ought* not do it in that way, though the negative attitude might be part of a causal explanation of why they did not do it that way on a particular occasion. To say that an individual person (or many persons) will engage an activity in a particular way is to predict behavior but not to explain why the person or persons *ought* to engage in an activity in a particular way. To say that an individual person (or many individuals) have engaged in a particular activity in a particular way is to record behavior; but that record of actions does not explain why a person *ought to have engaged* in that particular activity in that particular way. When restated in terms of individuals, their attitudes, and their behavior, the normativity tends to drop out. However, these points are far from decisive, and there are important and ongoing projects addressing social normativity in a nonreductionist fashion using the resources of methodological individualism.[3] How successful these projects are or will be remains an open question.

[3] For example, see Brennan et al., *Explaining Norms*, and Bicchieri, *Norms in the Wild*.

The artisanal model form of externalism highlights an additional problem facing methodological individualism that is often overlooked. Whether or not the normativity of all social roles is best understood on analogy with artisanal roles, many social roles *are* artisanal roles. And at least for artisanal roles, part of the normativity clearly derives from the conditions that must be satisfied for agents like us to effectively interact with and modify an independent external world, and that element of the source of the normativity clearly is not reducible to the attitudes and actions of individual human agents.[4] I think that the material "situatedness" of artisanal social roles carries over to other social roles and is an enlightening feature of the model. But, independently of this point, artisanal social roles seem to require a richer ontology than that offered by methodological individualism. And artisanal social roles are part of the explanandum of a theory of social role normativity. And this suggests a problem or limitation facing methodological individualism as a theory of social role normativity.

Because the artisanal form of externalism finds an aspect of the normativity of social roles to be situated, material, and world involving, it is committed to the rejection of methodological individualism. In order that the artisanal model work as a model for social role normativity, it requires terms that extend beyond the resources of methodological individualism. And as I noted, it is an open question whether certain features of the artisanal model can be successfully recast in individualist terms. To the extent that we are convinced by normative externalism and the artisanal model, we have reason to reject explanatory and ontological individualism. And, in addition, the obvious fact that at least some social roles, the artisanal ones, require norms that are situated, material, and world involving, give us prima facie reasons to think that it might be difficult for the methodological individualist programs to fully succeed as an account of social role normativity.

---

[4] Moreover, the work of many artisanal roles is not determined by individual attitudes but by what is required to sustain beings like us.

The rejection of methodological individualism brings with it the promise of a more complicated ontology of the social world and a richer set of explanatory resources. The conceptual complexity of the artisanal model raises questions about the relationship between the individual (the social position occupier) and the social role or, in other words, between the artisan, who has expertise, and the technique, the normatively assessable ways of doing something that comprise the social role to which the artisan ought to be responsive. An individual who occupies the social position of being a carpenter, who has that expertise, is thereby responsive to and evaluable by others according to normatively assessable techniques, or ways of building things out of wood around here. But what is the relationship between the individual and the social role?

The artisanal model illustrates the relationship between the social position occupier, the individual artisan, who has expertise, and the social role, which is comprised of normatively assessable techniques or ways of doing and making things. In the artisanal model the relationship between the individual (the social position occupier) and social role is expressed by the notions of expertise and technique. Expertise is an individual's ability or power to be responsive to the norms that constitute a technique (or set of techniques) in their actions as they engage in the normatively evaluable practices pertaining to a social role. The source of norms is the social role (or normatively evaluable techniques), but the very same norms are responded to and often realized in the activities of the expert. There are not two different sets of norms that constitute the art of carpentry in a specific context and locale, one comprising expertise and another different set comprising technique. Rather, there a way to be a carpenter around here that can exist either as the ability or power of an individual to be responsive to carpenter norms (expertise) or as normatively assessable ways of building things out of wood (technique). Expertise and technique display normative unity in the artisanal model. To see how this normative unity works in more detail we need to know more about expertise and technique.

## What Is a Technique?

Techniques are shared ways of working and acting within a community, and as such they are part of a community's social knowledge and shared practices. There are no private or individual techniques. Many techniques require interactions among cooperating individuals, each of whom are skilled in different ways; for example, the techniques involved in flying a plane between New York and London (the techniques employed by mechanics, pilots, air traffic controllers, etc.). Techniques require social interactions in the most literal sense of the term, as well as shared bodies of knowledge and know-how. But techniques are also realized in and by the actions and activities of individuals in the form of expertise. Expertise (or skill) refers to the technique possessed by an individual agent; it is a stable ability or power to perform an activity or function in a manner responsive to the relevant set of norms or techniques—to perform it badly, well, or in-between.[5] A technique is the public, shared practical knowledge condensed into the social role associated with a social position; it is normatively assessable know-how. Expertise refers to that very same public, shared practical knowledge—or normatively assessable know-how—as a power or ability of an individual.

Readers who are familiar with Aristotelian philosophy will, of course, recognize that technique derives from *techne*, a term that refers to artisanal activities like house building, and artistic activities like playing the lyre or the flute. For Aristotle, techniques like house building and cooking, which result in products, and techniques like playing a flute, which result in performances, are teachable and learnable methods of realizing a normatively evaluable function or work in activity. To be a housebuilder is to be able to use a technique to realize the work of building a house; the technique is a step-by-step process aimed at the end of producing

---

[5] Aristotle uses the phrase "*dunamis meta logou*" or "power with an account" to label what I am here calling "expertise." See *Met.* 1048a3.

a house. Although techniques often comprise a pattern of actions and activities, they are also flexible and sensitive to context and available materials. A good builder can deal with an unexpected ground contour, poor quality lumber, or a fussy client.

An Aristotelian technique has several additional features that are worth mentioning. In the first place, a technique is a kind of understanding or knowledge that passes from expert to apprentice.[6] There will be more on this important point in Chapter 5. Next, think of the various kinds of understanding that are gained in a culinary school—different ways of how one ought to do a vast number of tasks, some of which become habitual or ingrained. Moreover, fledgling chefs not only learn how they ought to do various tasks, but they also learn why they should be done a certain way. There are better and worse ways of doing things. Why weigh ingredients rather than use a volume measure? In Aristotelian idiolect, artisans know both the that and the why. They know what is to be done and why that is what is to be done. They have a *logos* or an explanation of why a given way of doing something is what is to be done.[7] They have a kind of practical understanding.[8]

---

[6] In "The Transmission of Skill," Will Small focuses on the transmission of skill in his critical discussion of intellectualist and nonintellectualist theories of skill and expertise. Small emphasizes the role played by practice, guided by experts in teaching skill, and he notes that, consequently, skills are inherently anti-individualist forms of practical knowledge.

[7] See Moss, "Right Reason in Plato and Aristotle," for an interpretation of "*logos*" as explanation in Plato and Aristotle. According to Moss, Aristotle describes *techne* as similar to the other kinds of intellectual excellence (practical wisdom and science) in being "with a *logos*" or—as Moss argues—with an explanation.

[8] The idea that techniques are kinds of practical knowledge is evidenced in Aristotle's theory of the four causes. Aristotle often identifies an artisan like a house builder as one of the causes, the origin of the motion or efficient cause, who originates the motion that ends with the product, the house. Sometimes, however, Aristotle says that the origin of motion or efficient cause is the technique or art in the artisan's soul. It is the artisan as having the art or the technique, that is, the expertise that the artisan possesses. These somewhat obscure comments express the point I have been making, which is that the technique of the house builder is a kind of practical knowledge in virtue of the possession of which the individual is a house builder.

There is a teachable body of culinary know-how that constitutes the technique of being a cook.[9] Much of that know-how consists of habituated abilities, but even this habitual know-how is context sensitive. Among other things, a good chef will know how to chop with a dull knife and make use of what is available at the local market. Of course, an individual need not go to culinary school to learn cooking technique; often learning takes place in restaurants or home kitchens through imitation and with varying degrees of direct instruction. The point is that the existence of techniques in human cultures presupposes that there are better and worse ways of realizing a function in activity or in a sequence of actions, and it also presupposes that the correct way is public and teachable. Someone who has mastered a technique has expertise in that field; experts can pass on techniques to apprentices.[10] And techniques like cooking are couched within complexes of practices (e.g., vegetarianism), institutions (e.g., the patriarchal family structure), and other features of social life (e.g., the dinner party, the farmer's market, or the soup kitchen). And, finally, techniques are both enabled and limited by material conditions; for example, what ingredients are available or practicable in a soup kitchen makes a difference to what cooking techniques are appropriate or best.

Given all the contextual features and material conditions that shape and influence cooking techniques, it is important to keep in mind that the notion of technique is inherently plural. So, while it is true to say that techniques are public and teachable, they are also multiple and deeply contextual. How best to prepare food in the home often differs significantly from how best to prepare it in institutional settings, like restaurants and soup kitchens, and that is the case even when we imagine the very same experienced and expert

---

[9] Of course, there are many teachable bodies of culinary know-how in many social contexts. The artisanal model is intended to capture the contextual nature of technique and expertise. Artisanal norms are always local; they are also plural.

[10] See Small, "Transmission," for a persuasive criticism of the view that being able to teach someone a skill is entirely independent of having the ability to do the skill.

chef in all three situations. And the numbers of technique variations multiply significantly once we factor in cultural differences. Despite the multiple variability of cooking techniques and their deeply contextual nature, however, cooking is an activity with normatively assessable methods that serve noninstrumental goods and excellences internal to the practice itself.

## What Is Expertise? Know-How and Know-Why

The Shelter Institute in Maine teaches people how to build post and beam houses, and its logo might have been written by Aristotle: Think. Build. Live. But it is not entirely clear what kind of thinking is relevant to acquiring expertise and deploying techniques. I have already mentioned that technique is properly thought of as a kind of knowledge that can be taught to apprentices by experts. And I have underlined the importance of activity as the expression of technique, by way of giving some content to the idea of social roles as ways of being human that are normatively assessable. But what is it to have expertise or know-how in some domain of human activity?

The modern debate over know-how and skill was inaugurated by Gilbert Ryle.[11] According to Ryle, "the intellectualist" mistakenly thinks that all knowledge, including skills and expertise, is knowing that, or propositional knowledge. For example, the intellectualist might think that expertise in chess consists in knowing the rules and tactics of the game, and then applying them skillfully.

---

[11] Ryle's discussion of the independence and priority of know-how and the subsequent debate between intellectualists and nonintellectualists is important in highlighting the phenomena of skill and expertise in our practical agency. My neo-Aristotelian perspective on expertise focuses on a different question in arguing for the explanatory resources of expertise in this chapter, and by exploring the significance of the transmission of expertise in the next chapter.

Famously, Ryle argued for the independence—and priority—of know-how over knowing that.[12] For Ryle, knowing how to build a house is expressed in skillful activity and is not, as the intellectualist thinks, a matter of applying a set of propositions or instructions. Ryle's discussion of the independence and priority of know-how in relation to knowledge that, and the subsequent debate between followers of Ryle and his critics, is complex, interesting, and somewhat tangential to my project. My neo-Aristotelian perspective on expertise or know-how does not directly address or center upon the epistemological issues and causal issues pertinent to the disagreement between Ryle and his critics.[13] My focus is on the normative aspect of expertise, and the way in which the notion of expertise allows us to explain what someone is doing and why they are doing it the way they are doing it by pointing to the norms that a person with that expertise ought to be responsive to. Expertise on my view is knowing how to do something the way one ought to do it around here. The expertise does not cause anyone to perform a particular action, but it does explain the person's actions in terms of the norms they ought to be responsive to because of their expertise and the social position they occupy.

So, both sides of the traditional debate over know-how leave something important out. Aristotelian expertise is a kind of know-how that is responsive to the norms that imbue the relevant techniques and that are expressed in normatively evaluable activity—but even that is not the whole story. Techniques are normatively evaluable ways of doing or making something, but they

---

[12] For a recent criticism of Ryle's regress argument against intellectualism see Stanley, *Know How*. For a critical evaluation of Stanley's criticism of Ryle, see Friedland, "Problems with Intellectualism." Small argues that it is a mistake to interpret Ryle in terms of the debate between intellectualism and anti-intellectualism and that Ryle's aim "is to give an account of the intelligence of intelligent action" ("Ryle on the Explanatory Role of Knowledge How" 57).

[13] See Will Small's "Transmission" for insightful discussion of how the resources in the Aristotelian and commonsense notion of expertise can be lost in an exclusive focus on the issues and questions posed by Ryle and the subsequent philosophical conversation.

also include the ability to give an explanation (a *logos*) of what you are doing. So, when a chef has cooking expertise, for example, they are both able to make cakes the right way and—if asked and perhaps on reflection—able to explain why they are doing the various things they are doing. An expert baker knows how one ought to frost a cake and why it is important to do a crumb coat. Expertise is a kind of know-how that includes understanding or the ability to give an explanation of what one is doing. It is know-how plus know-why, where the latter refers to why it is done this way around here. The phrase "around here" deserves underlining because it expresses that artisanal norms, and hence social roles norms, are always local and situated.

The addition of know-why to know-how or expertise creates possibilities for change and improvement in techniques. An expert chef knows how to make a souffle that rises every time, which requires that the eggs are perfectly separated. But the expert chef also knows why the eggs must be perfectly separated. No "goldfish" are allowed in the egg whites because the fat in egg yolks impedes the formation of bubbles in egg whites. Because expertise includes both know-how and know-why, the artisan is able to criticize or to improve the techniques and norms to which they are responsive. Perhaps there is a better way you ought to proceed to keep the goldfish out?

Ideally a person who has taken the course at the Shelter Institute in Maine on post and beam construction has gained both know-how and know-why. When they build a house, they do so in a manner responsive to post and beam building norms, and they also can explain why these norms are correct. They are taught how to engage in the activities of house building in a manner responsive to local house building norms, and also they learn why the various activities and materials are the right ones for the job at hand given those local norms. This know-why allows a student to be flexible to context and to substitute materials if necessary or to modify their technique in new circumstances. Expertise rests on the notion of technique, which is the idea that there are normatively assessable ways of engaging in human activities or realizing social roles around here. Techniques are normatively assessable and open to critique precisely because they incorporate both know-how and know-why. They are ways of engaging in human activities that are amenable to explanation and thereby encode understanding and—because of the element of explanation—are open to rational criticism, debate, and change. I discuss the resources of the artisanal model for norm critique, debate, and change further in Chapter 5. There I describe how the transmission of expertise on the artisanal model via habituation and imitation helps to explain two aspects of social role norms. First, the artisanal learning model helps explain why social role norms persist and are resistant to change. But the very same process of habituation also provides the materials for the rational critique of social role norms and social role change.

While it is true that we often become skillful in a domain by practice and through habituation, displays of technique and expert activities are not rote and mechanical behaviors. As Julia Annas observes concerning Aristotle's comparison between virtue and skill (*techne*), "The analogy between virtue and skill is not meant to suggest that virtue is an unreflective habit of practiced action" ("Virtue as a Skill" 227). Rather, by drawing a comparison between virtue and skill, Aristotle exploits the intellectual and practical structure of a skill, and in particular the fact that artisans have both know-how and know-why. And this is true even when an experienced artisan acts spontaneously and without explicit deliberation. The point is that the artisan could explain what they are doing and why they are doing it in this context. The expert can teach the novice. As Aristotle puts it, "It is a sign of the man who knows that he can teach, and therefore we think art [*techne*] more truly knowledge than experience is; for artists can teach and men of experience cannot" (*Met.*, I 1, 981b6–9).

Let's step back for a moment, look at the big picture, and see how the pieces fit together. How are technique and expertise related to one another in our normatively evaluable social practices? Social roles are realized in techniques and in expertise. Techniques are normatively evaluable ways of doing or making things; they are shared ways of acting and interacting, shared ways of realizing social roles in a context. And they are understood to be so by members of the community. Expertise is the ability of an individual to act in a way that is responsive to normatively assessable techniques or ways of doing things. Hence, technique and expertise are ontologically intertwined and conceptually interdependent. They are two facets of the very same thing; they are both ways of realizing a social role. Without transmissible technique there would be no individual development of expertise; without individual expertise there would be no responsiveness to normatively evaluable techniques. Hence, if there were no techniques there would be no expertise and vice versa. Social roles are neither individual skills alone, independent of a shared social meaning and context, nor are they techniques alone, independent of their realization in the expertise and activities of individuals. To express this idea, I borrow the useful term "connective tissue" from Davidson and Kelly to describe social roles as ways of being human that knit individuals into a meaningful social fabric. "In this way, social norms form a soft but durable connective tissue that binds individuals to groups via cycling loops of mutual influence" (13).

## Social Role Change, Criticism, and Creation

The issue of social role change is complex in part because of the normative unity and flow between technique and expertise in the artisanal model. Expertise (or know-how) is an individual's ability or power to be responsive to the public and shared techniques that are ways of doing or making something. For this reason, because the individual and the social role are normatively intermeshed, change in norms can "flow" in either direction. When what a social role demands changes, the normative obligation of individuals who occupy the associated social position also changes. But the flow is not only in one direction. Social roles are open to pressure from individuals, who might reject (or reshape) a norm either because they are nonconforming types, or because they find the norm incompatible with other social norm obligations—or for some other reason. Perhaps since they understand why it is better to do x in situation y, they might come to think that it is better yet to do z in situation y. These individual nonconformers or critics can, under certain circumstances, change the normative contours of a particular social role or cluster of social roles. Norm change can flow in this way from individual(s) to social role. I use the phrase "normative flow" deliberately in an attempt to capture the complexity of this process, which might include eddies, backflow, rivulets, and whirlpools.

In Chapter 2 I argued that one reason that normative externalism is preferable to internalism is that it can accommodate the phenomenon of social role nonconformers—people who are responsive to and evaluable under a social role, but who reject it—either in part or as a whole. Social role nonconformers are an important phenomenon to be able to explain, and it is an especially important phenomenon in the context of understanding how social role norms can change. On the externalist account a person is responsive to and evaluable under a norm just by virtue of occupying a social position that includes that norm in the social role. For the externalist, the social role nonconformer criticizes or rejects a norm that they are responsive to and evaluable under, which is at the heart of nonconforming behavior. It is why nonconforming behavior often takes courage. You cannot be a nonconforming agent in relation to norms that you do not stand under in the first place. But the internalist cannot appeal to the social position occupancy to ground the obligation, and so this explanation of social role nonconformers is not available to them. The internalist cannot explain how the norms get traction for the nonconformer who, by definition, does not prefer or self-legislate the norm in question. This is a clear explanatory win for the externalist account of the source of social role normativity.

However, while social role nonconformers are best explained by normative externalism, it just isn't clear that they are fully compatible with certain features of the artisanal model. The triad of function, technique, and expertise describes social roles in terms that seem inhospitable to change and to the formation of social norm critics or social role nonconformers. To see why, consider the artisanal model and how it represents the transmission of technique and the development of expertise in an individual. The picture is of an apprentice gradually developing expertise or know-how in a craft through habituation, imitation, and guided practice. This process helps explain the resistance to change of social role norms, their "stickiness." Habituation and imitation describe processes that retain and replicate social norms during the process of transmission. But now it becomes a puzzle how an individual nonconformer or norm innovator could develop. Where would the materials or perspective for critique of the social role or the raw materials for normative innovation come from? If a sense of excellence is cultivated with the development of expertise, then the agent seems to be trapped within a particular web of norms. What resources does the artisanal model of social role normativity have for critical or innovative selves, including nonconforming social agents?

The resources of the artisanal model for social change might also seem limited due to its externalist orientation—the very feature that allows it to explain the phenomenon of social norm nonconformers. If the source of social role normativity is in the social position occupancy, or in other words if the source of the normativity lies partially in the structure of the social world itself, then it might seem particularly puzzling how social norm change is possible. And we might wonder, in addition, how individuals who stand under the norms could have a part to play in changing social roles. But, as I mentioned earlier, an adequate theory of social role normativity ought to be able to explain both the persistence and resistance to change of social role norms, and the ability of individuals to criticize the norms they stand under, and to engage in normative self-creation.

In the next two chapters I focus on the resources of the artisanal model to allow the individual a role in social norm criticism and in normative self-creation. In Chapter 5 I develop the resources of the artisanal model to explain how social norm criticism is possible by individuals who stand under the norms in question. It is true that the transmission of expertise via habituation, imitation, and guided practice on the artisanal model helps to explain the persistence and resistance to change of social role norms. But, as I explain, it is also true that the very same process of norm transmission and the development of expertise creates the possibility for both norm criticism and norm innovation. Then, in Chapter 6, I explain how externalism and the artisanal model have the conceptual resources to explain the way that normative self-creation might occur in an individual. Indeed, I argue that the artisanal model and externalism can unravel the paradox of self-creation, but that familiar forms of internalism fail to do so. The paradox of self-creation arises when an individual undergoes a transformative normative change and becomes a "new" self. But how can this happen? Either the person is simply developing norms they already have in which case it is not a transformative normative change. Or the person acquires a genuinely new norm in which case it is a puzzle how that happens. Our by now familiar internalist theories are unable to resolve this paradox adequately, but externalism and the artisanal model can unravel the paradox. Since normative self-creation is one of the phenomena to be explained, this is another consideration that favors externalism and the artisanal model.

# 5
# Habituation, Imitation, and the Critical Self

Thus far my focus has been on developing an externalist account of the source of social role normativity, and an externalist explanation for why particular individuals are responsive to and evaluable under specific norms using the artisanal model. Normative externalism is a perspective that brings into focus the normative structure of the social world, and the way in which it shapes, impinges upon, and infuses our agency. And understanding the externalist normativity of social roles using Afunctions allows us to explain the source of their normativity by modelling them on artisanal social roles. In particular, it provides a way of understanding, via our social position occupancies, how and why we are responsive to and evaluable under certain norms. Just as there are techniques and expertise associated with being a cook or a doctor, so, too there are techniques and expertise associated with being a mother or being an academic or being a president. To be a mother or an academic or a president is to be responsive to and evaluable under the norms that constitute these social roles by virtue of your social position occupancy.

But we are not always positively oriented to the social norms that we are responsive to and evaluable under—nor should we be. Social norms and social roles oppress as well as enable. Just as interesting and as important to understand as our obligation to the norms we stand under is our ability to criticize them. Critical selves are individuals who engage rational criticism of the social roles that

*Social Goodness.* Charlotte Witt, Oxford University Press. © Oxford University Press 2023.
DOI: 10.1093/oso/9780197574799.003.0005

they are responsive to and evaluable under by virtue of the social positions they occupy. Although responsive to and evaluable under a norm, critical selves are also able to engage in rational criticism of them. Critical selves are among the phenomena to be explained in an adequate theory of social role normativity. Hence an adequate theory of social role normativity requires the logical space for the possibility of critical selves and an explanation of how they could develop.

In Chapter 2 I pointed out one reason that externalism about social role normativity was preferable to normative internalism, namely that externalism could accommodate the phenomenon of social role nonconformers. According to normative externalism, social role nonconformers do not adhere to one or more of the norms that constitute the social role that they stand under by virtue of their social position occupancy. While not all noncomformers are critical selves who engage in rational criticism of the social roles they stand under, and not all critical selves are nonconformers in their behavior, there is significant overlap between the two groups. Hence, an adequate explanation of all three—critical selves, nonconformers, and critical selves who are nonconforming—are a requirement for an acceptable theory of social role normativity. In this chapter I explain how the artisanal model can accommodate and find space for critical selves, including those who are nonconformers.

Let me sum up the situation thus far. In Chapter 2, as part of my initial argument for externalism about the source of social role normativity, I considered the claim that normative internalism provides a better perspective for criticism of social roles—president, academic, mother—than externalism. I pointed out that in fact internalism and externalism are on a par because both require additional materials, concepts, or principles to formulate and ground ethical or political critique of social roles. Neither explanation of the source of social role normativity can engage normative critique of social roles without supplement. Internalism and externalism, as explanations of the source of social role normativity, are on a par as far as the critique of social roles goes.

But this verdict leaves us with an important question. How do agents occupying social positions—president, academic, mother—develop critical attitudes toward the norms to which they are responsive and under which they are evaluable? This is the problem of the critical self. The possibility of critical selves is particularly important in relation to the social roles we stand under, since all of us live our lives in and through these normatively inflected ways of being human. And many of us find specific norms to be oppressive and in need of change. And others of us consider some social roles—as a whole—to be entirely unacceptable.

In this chapter I develop the idea that the artisanal model contains significant resources for critical selves. The artisanal model of social norm acquisition provides a plausible explanation of how individuals who stand under norms by virtue of their social position occupancy can nonetheless be critical of them. It is important to underline at the outset that an adequate theory of social role normativity must be able to explain how we develop critical selves. The ability to explain how critical selves develop is not an add-on to a theory of social role normativity; it is an intrinsic component of an adequate theory.

We can distinguish critical selves in relation to the range and target of their critical attitudes. An agent's critical attitude might focus on a single norm (or perhaps several norms) that constitute the social role. These are the reformers. For example, a woman might criticize (and perhaps try to change or to improve) the prevalent gendered norms of appearance in her culture. Think of the way in which lingerie advertisements now reflect new attitudes toward socially acceptable body types as a result of the activism of gender appearance nonconformers. Or the agent's critical attitude might be global and directed toward the complete elimination of a social role. These are the eliminativists. For example, a person might be a gender eliminativist and think that the world would just be a better place without gender roles of any kind—or at least without binary gender roles.[1] While reformers and eliminativists differ with regard to the breadth or range of their critical attitudes, the elements that explain their ability to be critical selves are the same.

Explaining the development of critical selves seems particularly tricky for the artisanal model of social role normativity. On the face of it, the framework of function, technique, and expertise appears to lack the resources to explain how it is that agents might be critical of the social roles associated with the positions that they occupy and to which they are responsive. How can the Afunction view of social roles accommodate critical selves with the resources, perspective, and critical "space" to be either reformers or eliminators?

The challenge deepens when we consider one aspect of the artisanal model, which I have not yet emphasized. The artisanal model suggests a process of social norm acquisition that might seem particularly difficult to square with the existence of critical selves. Artisanal social role expertise develops through imitation, habituation, and guided practice; you learn how to cook or how to play the guitar by practicing, by imitating role models, and by explicit instruction and correction from experts. These activities result in know-how, which is a power or ability to act in a norm responsive manner. A person learns by guided practice, habituation, and imitation, and then knows how to cook or how to teach or how to apply makeup. It is reasonable to wonder where in this picture we find resources for criticism (or improvement) of practices or norms or a perspective from which to criticize global sets of practices or, in other words, the social roles themselves.

Two aspects of the artisanal model provide resources for critical selves both for reformers and for eliminators. The first resource

---

[1] For an influential definition of gender terms that is eliminativist, see Haslanger, "Gender and Race: (What) Are They? (What) Do We Want Them to Be?"

originates in the way we acquire know-how or expertise, namely through habituation. As we will see, habituation is a process of developing know-how that is normatively rich and complex. It instills both a particular kind of expertise, and it also inculcates a habit of excellence that transcends any particular application or skill. We come to see that there are things we ought to do and ought to aspire to regardless of inclination. There is a normative texture and depth to the know-how we develop through habituation, and this provides one resource for the development of critical selves. As it turns out the "practical expertise" developed by habituation can enable critical reflection rather than only stifling it.[2]

I mentioned a second resource for critical selves in Chapter 4, which is that a technique is both know-how and know-why. The latter aspect of technique allows for critical assessment (and improvement) of the individual norms that comprise a social role and, in some circumstances, of the social role itself. Because an apprentice acquires know-how and know-why through habituation, they have the resources to improve and to criticize the social role they occupy. Indeed, people who have expertise, who have developed know-how and know-why, are often the source of the most telling normative critique and the best normative innovation. Properly understood, habituation develops practical expertise, which includes both know-how and know-why. So, the expert in doing something is also an expert in how to criticize what they are doing and how to improve what it is they are doing. Despite our initial doubts, it turns out that the artisanal model of social role normativity provides rich resources for critical selves.

---

[2] Julia Annas draws a useful distinction between practical expertise and routine habituation. Practical expertise is a handy term that unites the know-how aspect of expertise and the know-why aspect. See "Practical Expertise."

## Skill Acquisition and the Critical Self

How do we develop know-how, skill, or expertise? And where precisely in this story is there room for the development of critical selves? Unsurprisingly, the general approach to skill acquisition I favor is Aristotelian. Aristotle famously claims that moral virtue, like other skills and expertise, develops through a process of habituation. However, the process of habit formation by means of practice is, for Aristotle, more than simply Aristotle's account of virtue acquisition; it is also part of what virtue is. Unlike Plato in the *Meno*, who prioritizes the "What is it?" question concerning virtue and distinguishes it sharply from the question of how we become virtuous, Aristotle weaves a discussion of how virtue originates into his discussion of what virtue is. He clearly does not think that we need to determine, or could determine, what virtue is independently of the question of how we become virtuous. More about the details of this process and its critical resources in a moment.

But first let's consider two alternative explanations of skill acquisition that also use an artisanal model to explain the acquisition of social norms: Dreyfus's explanation, which draws on Heideggerian themes, and Sterelny's apprentice learning model.[3] As we will see, Dreyfus's influential account of skill acquisition entirely lacks the resources to explain the development of critical selves. In contrast, Sterelny's apprentice learning model has resources to explain critical selves, but since his focus is on the transmission and preservation of artisanal technique rather than the development of the ability to engage rational criticism of it, these resources are not developed. Nonetheless it is useful to consider these two important descriptions of social norm acquisition modelled on skill acquisition to determine what is missing.

---

[3] See Dreyfus, *Skillful Coping*, and Sterelny, *The Evolved Apprentice*. Of course, there are many other important accounts of skill acquisition. I focus on the important explanations of Sterelny and Dreyfus for purposes of exposition, comparison, and contrast.

Hubert Dreyfus developed an account of skill acquisition that draws on Heidegger and the phenomenological tradition.[4] According to Dreyfus, the process of skill acquisition begins with detached rule following by the apprentice, moves through stages of more and more complex maxim or rule following, and ends with competence.[5] The competent person must decide which rules to follow rather than merely following rules dictated by others. But whether the rules are handed to you (a typical child) or decided upon by you (a typical adult), rule following only leads to competence and not expertise: "In general, if one seeks to follow general rules one will not get beyond competence."[6] For Dreyfus, expertise issues in "an immediate, intuitive response to each situation" or—to use his term—skillful coping.[7] Skillful coping, or acting in the flow, is a term of art Dreyfus uses to refer to the exercise of nonrepresentational know-how. It is a state with which many of us are familiar, which happens when we are fully absorbed in a task and simply do the right thing without thought or hesitation.

Dreyfus models the development of ethical know-how on his account of skill acquisition: "*If* the skill model we have proposed is correct, then, insofar as ethical comportment is a form of expertise, we should expect it to exhibit a developmental structure similar to that which we have described" (*Skillful Coping* 189).

For Dreyfus, ethical comportment can be usefully viewed as a skill, and, as with other skills, he thinks we start by following explicit social rules and end—sometimes—in the zone of immediate and spontaneous decision or action: "Also with enough experience

---

[4] Ironically enough, Dreyfus roots his phenomenology of skill acquisition in Aristotle's notion of *techne*. Dreyfus reports that Heidegger was working on the notion of *techne* when developing the ideas that inspired his account of how we develop skills. See *Background Practices*, page 29. However, Dreyfus's phenomenology of skill acquisition, which centers detached rule following rather than habituation and imitation, is not Aristotelian.

[5] In some places Dreyfus adds the stage of proficiency between competence and expertise. See *Skillful Coping*, pages 187–188.

[6] Dreyfus, *Background Practices*, 31.

[7] Ibid., 32.

and willingness to take risks, some children grow up to be ethical experts who have learned to tell the truth or lie spontaneously, depending upon the situation, without appeal to rules and maxims" (*Background Practices* 32).

But neither phase of this process provides materials for norm criticism or for the development of critical selves. The phase of explicit rule following provides no space or perspective for criticism, and neither does the final phase of being fully absorbed in a task. It is just unclear that Dreyfus could explain the development of critical selves in terms of his explanation of the development of expertise and ethical know-how. Indeed, Dreyfus explicitly denies that an expert (whether an artisan or a moral expert), can explain why they did what they did (*Background Practices* 37). So, Dreyfus's account lacks even the potential for the development of critical selves provided by the know-why that accompanies know-how on the artisanal model.

Dreyfus does address the problem of ethical and artistic innovation by distinguishing among three kinds of experts. The conventional expert intuits what is appropriate to do or say in a context. The *phronimos* goes beyond mere convention when facing conflicts and, in doing so, realizes new possibilities. Finally, the "radical innovator" is drawn to act in ways that "will open up new forms of intelligibility and new possibilities for action" (*Skillful Coping* 12). Given Dreyfus's explanation of skill acquisition, however, it is difficult to see how the creative experts would arise. They seem to spring forth like mushrooms.

Moreover, Dreyfus's description seems to get the phenomenology of skill acquisition wrong. While some skill acquisition, like learning to play chess, might begin with learning rules, most skills begin with guided practice, imitation, and habit formation. Another reason to be skeptical of Dreyfus is his idea that skillful coping is incompatible with the idea that expertise comprises both know-how and know-why. That we experience skillful coping or acting in the flow is compatible with the view that expertise is comprised of know-how and know-why. Often when we act spontaneously we can also (retroactively) explain why we did what we did. So, acting in the flow is compatible with expertise comprising both know-how and know-why. But Dreyfus's actual account of skill acquisition does not provide us with a description that has the resources to explain the development of critical or creative selves.

Now let's consider a second important description of norm acquisition that has more resources for the development of critical selves. In *The Evolved Apprentice*, Kim Sterelny endorses the "apprentice learning model," which explains human learning in terms of two elements—socially guided trial and error, and practice (xii). For Sterelny, the apprentice learning model characterizes the distinctively human way of passing on accumulated technical knowledge between generations. However, the apprentice learning model also "has broad application beyond formal apprenticeship in highly skilled craft guilds" (36). In particular, children need to learn how to navigate the normative structure of their social worlds, and Sterelny explains how they accomplish this using the apprentice learning model: "But children come to learn not just the tools of their ecological trade and characteristics of their local world. They had to acquire the distinctive language, mores, customs, attitudes, beliefs, and public symbols of their group" (152).

Sterelny adopts a neo-Aristotelian perspective in proposing that we can explain the development of moral competence or moral know-how in children similar to the way in which we explain skill acquisition: "The acquisition of moral competence depends on mechanisms that are similar to, and are modified from, those that explain skill acquisition" (152).[8] Sterelny adds, "Children learn the norms of their social world by acting in their social world. They learn by doing" (170). Further, Sterelny notes that children do not

---

[8] Sterelny refers to "mechanisms" and his interest is in causal questions broadly construed. But, so is Aristotle in his discussion of habituation; it is a process that instills the virtues.

merely need to learn what my people do (an empirical generalization) but also what they ought to do in a given circumstance as part of the community. Children develop a responsive normative attitude. Like Aristotle, Sterelny finds a model for the acquisition of social norms in the apprentice system of learning found in arts and crafts. Also, like Aristotle, he places emphasis on activity, on doing, and on habituation.[9]

Artisanal expertise is a rich blend of explicit and implicit information. As Sterelny puts it:

> A skilled craftsperson has a good deal of explicit information at his or her fingertips: rules of thumb, the lore of the trade. This explicit, articulated, detachable information co-exists and interacts with pattern recognition capacities; well-tuned habits; information that can be made explicit but only with the right prompts; know-how. The distinction between explicit and tacit is not sharp: a cabinetmaker may be able to explain, say, the reasons why she rejected one source of raw materials in favor of another, but only slowly and partially, reconstructing the decision rather than reporting on it. (169)

A skilled cabinetmaker can explain why she used a particular wood, but this information is often tacit rather than explicit. I argue below that the know-why aspect of expertise provides an important resource for the criticism of existing social roles. Indeed, I will argue that excellence in carpentry and the accompanying disposition to excellence more generally allows for the internal criticism of the dominant norms of carpentry and of the role of carpenters as such. But, for Sterelny, the important point is that artisanal expertise includes both explicit and implicit factors, and not that

---

[9] My description of Sterelny's fascinating discussion of the apprentice learning model, its application to learning social norms, and its centrality to being human is necessarily incomplete and limited in focus. I recommend consulting *The Evolved Apprentice* for the full story.

knowing-why can be a springboard for the criticism of existing norms or the development of new norms and roles.

Hence, while there is much to like about Sterelny's apprentice learning model for the acquisition of social norms, it does not include any explicit discussion of resources that might explain the development of critical selves. He does not ask how it is possible to critique one's own social skills and the norms to which one is responsive. The intergenerational transmission of artisanal techniques via apprenticeship might provide a useful model for the development of normative know-how, but it is incomplete because there is no clear provision within Sterelny's artisanal model for the development of critical selves. And, as I noted above, the development of critical selves is an essential element in normative skill acquisition, and so an account of how this happens is an important part of an explanation of social norm acquisition.

Although they differ markedly in the details of their explanations of how expertise develops, both Dreyfus and Sterelny share the Aristotelian idea of modeling normative learning and expertise on artisanal learning and expertise. They are also similar in that neither explains the acquisition of normative expertise in a way that explicitly includes provision for the existence of critical selves, although Sterelny's account contains the raw materials needed for their inclusion. But if I am right and the development of responsiveness to norms includes the possibility of criticism as an integral component, then something crucial is missing. We can find the missing element in Aristotle's account of the acquisition of know-how or expertise through habituation and imitation.

## What Is Habituation?

First, a little terminology. The term standardly translated as "habituation" is *ethismos,* and it just means "an inculcation of *ethe.*" Now *ethe* is a term usually translated as "habits," but—importantly for my argument—the term is broad and also connotes "customs, mores, accepted ways of behavior, usages" (Broadie 103). In contrast, a habit is simply a settled or regular practice, especially one that is hard to give up—like rising at 6 am every morning, or obsessively checking Facebook. Aristotle's *ethe* are not simply habits like these, but rather inculcated (and socially accepted) complex patterns of activity with normative content. So, the translation of *ethe* as "habits" both includes too much and fails to capture the rich social and normative connotations of the term. In fact, in some contexts, we might correctly translate *ethe* as "social norms" and *ethismos* as the "inculcation of social norms." Having flagged these translation issues and possibilities, however, I will continue to use the translation of *ethe* as "habit" and *ethismos* as "habituation," because they are part of an inherited and shared Aristotelian idiolect. These translations are part of the *ethe* of Aristotle interpretation.

In centering the role of habituation in the development of moral virtue, Aristotle often draws a comparison with the development of artisanal techniques: "The things we have to learn before we can do, we learn by doing, e.g., men become builders by building and lyre-players by playing the lyre; so too we become just by doing just acts, temperate by doing temperate acts, brave by doing brave acts" (*EN*, 1103a32–b2).

Hallvard Fossheim usefully supplies some detail by describing the role of imitation or *mimesis* in the process of habituation or learning by doing: "Children and young people develop their character by actively engaging in mimesis of others who function as models for them. The child does as others do and learns to become a certain sort of person by emulating the actions and manners of others" (111). Indeed, Aristotle uses the comparison between learning to be virtuous and learning how to engage an artisanal activity to defuse a paradox shadowing his view, namely how one can perform virtuous actions *before* being virtuous. Aristotle points out that this is how we develop a wide range of expertise and techniques, by doing what it is that we are learning to do. Often this involves imitation of experts. Whether or not Aristotle is successful in diffusing the paradox is open to scholarly disagreement.

Habituation or enculturation requires practice and imitation to develop expertise, but it is important to see that the process has two distinguishable outcomes. In the artisanal context what is developed when we acquire a particular kind of know-how, such as how to build a house, is both reflective of the norms of a particular context and culture (e.g., contemporary Japanese architecture), and a general habituation toward, and appreciation of, excellence. In the case of the virtues, habituation inculcates both an ability to do what should be done around here, and an appreciation for "the noble." As Sarah Broadie puts it, "Learning that there are things which one is expected to do even when all concerned are aware that one does not feel like doing them is perhaps the only way we have of learning from scratch that there are things worth doing and aiming for that are not immediately pleasant. This is our way into an active sense of 'noble'" (109). Through habituation and by imitation, we develop concrete, particular, and culturally situated normative know-how: how things ought to be done around here. But we also develop a habituated appreciation of "rightness," or what-ought-to-be-done, more generally. This dual outcome provides the preconditions for critique of particular norms (e.g., gendered norms of appearance) and the global critique of social roles (e.g., gendered social roles). The habituated general orientation toward excellence provides a perspective from which to criticize particular social role norms. In what way does covering one's hair or wearing stilettos realize or manifest our habituation toward excellence in a more generalized sense? Why engage in these local practices? Why be responsive to this norm? This kind of question brings us to the second resource for critical selves, which is intimately bound up with the notion of artisanal expertise or know-how.

The second resource for criticism in the Afunction model is the idea, introduced in Chapter 4, that the artisan's know-how is accompanied by know-why. The artisan's ability to adapt to new situations and challenges is part of her expertise, as is the ability to criticize current practices and norms. Adaptation, improvement, and criticism are enhanced and secured by the artisan's grasp of why it is that certain things are to be done (in a context) and why they are not to be done (in another situation). How exactly does the addition of know-why add to our ability to be critical selves? Recall the earlier example from Sterelny of the carpenter who chooses—without reflection—a certain wood to make a cabinet, but who could explain—if asked—why she chose the wood. Artisanal expertise is comprised of both know-how (the original decision) and know-why (the later explanation). As Sterelny notes, often the reasons why a given artisanal decision or choice was made will be tacit and initially inarticulate. The motivation for the articulation of the know-why in a situation is often the general orientation toward excellence. A sense of the excellent, which is inculcated through habituation, can motivate us to raise the question of why we should do what is required around here, which in turn leads to an explication of the reasons, or know-why, and that leads in turn to the possibility of critique. This line of thought could prompt, in certain circumstances, the thought that another type of wood or building process might be better and that, in this circumstance, the use of another wood or process would be better. As it turns out Sterelny's notion of tacit or implicit reasons for an artisanal decision can lay the groundwork for the development of critical selves.

Applying the artisanal model to the context of social role norms, we can see that the expert mother or skilled professor or excellent president has both know-how and know-why, which enables them to engage in critical thinking and in critical discourse with others. Having and giving reasons for one's actions is central to being a critical self. For example, through debate with colleagues (or inspired by students), a professor might come to see that the goal of teaching and teaching excellence is better realized by the "inverted classroom" technique than by the traditional "sage on the stage" approach. Habituation toward excellence (in the double sense explained above) works with the critical resources of know-why. Reformers can gradually change the normative profile of a social role in this manner by questioning the excellence or utility of a particular norm or norms, even one to which they are currently responsive.

## Habituation, Reward, and Punishment

My description of skill acquisition through the process of habituation does not mention any role played by rewards or punishment, although both the notions of guided practice and imitation might include corrections of the novice during the process of habituation. However, in some circumstances, punishment and coercion are central to the process of habituation. In situations of involuntary labor or exploitation it seems likely that punishment or the threat of punishment plays a role in coercing individuals to develop (and to employ) know-how or expertise. For example, consider a child who is an apprentice rug-maker or a young Afghan girl learning to align with oppressive, gendered comportment and attire. Corporal punishment is still widespread in families in the United States to punish behavior that exceeds or transgresses perceived social norms. And rewards might also be used to prompt practice and the other modes of habituation. How do rewards and punishment fit into the Aristotelian picture of skill acquisition, and hence norm acquisition, on the artisanal model?

In response to this question, it is important to distinguish the causal factors that prompt imitation and practice (which might include both reward and punishment, both tacit and explicit) from the activities that constitute the habituation process: imitation and guided practice. The latter activities are constitutive of artisanal learning and the acquisition of expertise and, by extension, the acquisition of social norm expertise. Recall that Aristotle includes how expertise and virtue arises in us via habituation in his definition of what expertise or virtue is. If we conflate the activities that transmit expertise with the rewards and punishments that might motivate us to engage with these activities, we will not have provided an explanation or model for social norm acquisition. The normativity of social norms does not reduce to a cost-benefit analysis in terms of sanctions avoided and rewards gained. It is not even clear that rewards and punishments are always psychological motivators to act in accordance with social norms, since people do so even in situations of total anonymity. The question of why a mother ought to take care of her children is different from the psychological question of what causes her to take care of her children, though that a mother ought to do so might be a causal factor in her decision. For this reason, it is important to distinguish between the rewards and punishments that might cause someone to engage in the activities that develop expertise, and the activities of habituation, imitation and guided practice that constitute the development of expertise. There is an important difference between acting on a cost-benefit analysis and acting in a manner responsive to the norms that constitute expertise (whether artisanal or social). Developing expertise, which is an individual's ability to act in a norm responsive manner, explains both why an individual ought to respond to certain norms and why that individual might be critical of one or more of those very same norms.

## Conclusion

I have been exploring the idea that the Afunction explanation of social role normativity provides significant resources for the development of critical selves. But I actually think this way of putting the point is a bit misleading. It's not just that there are resources for criticism in the Afunction explanation of social role normativity, but rather that expertise and the ability to criticize are interwoven with one another. The very same people who are most expert are often those whose critical thinking on a practice is most valuable. Consider for a moment the difference between Yo-Yo Ma criticizing the norms inspiring a cello performance and me engaging in the same normative criticism. Which criticism would be more powerful, subtle, and on target, not to mention most persuasive? The Afunction interpretation of social roles allows us to make the same point about social roles quite generally. Rather than stifle and impair social criticism, creativity, or norm change, expertise can enable it.

The person with expertise can make accurate, detailed, and persuasive criticisms of the norms governing a practice to which they are responsive. Of course, the social role critic must have genuine expertise. I have been assuming throughout this chapter that the trifecta of activity or function, expertise, and technique exist in the context of social role normativity. And I think that we have good reason to think that they do exist as structural elements in our social world. We have good reason to think that genuine experts exist who are particularly well situated to criticize the social norms and social roles in relation to which they have expertise. And this is true even if there is robust disagreement over who the genuine experts are. This debate goes back to Plato's *Gorgias* and won't be resolved here.

I have argued that the Afunction explanation of the source of social role normativity has significant resources for critical selves, for agents who are critical of various aspects of the social roles they are responsive to and evaluable under. Critical selves include social role nonconformers, who have a central role to play in changing social norms and expectations. However, there is another important aspect of human experience that seems incompatible with my externalist explanation of social role normativity using the artisanal model, and that is the existence of our deep practical commitments and our powers of self-creation. Is the artisanal model of social role normativity compatible with what I will call "the creative self"?

# 6
# Self-Creation and Transformation

"[Aristotle's] point is that we become the people we make ourselves." (126)

Agnes Callard

We all engage with multiple social positions at a time and over time. Indeed, the social positions we occupy ground our social lives and activities. They help to shape the normative contours of our social agency. As I outlined in the first three chapters of this book, understanding social roles in terms of the artisanal model provides a promising externalist model for explaining the source and character of social role normativity. In Chapter 5 I described how the artisanal model also provides resources to explain the development of critical selves, both those who criticize particular social role norms, and those who advocate the elimination of social roles. Social role eliminators are those who find either individual norms or norms taken together so repugnant that they argue for the elimination of the role entirely. Social role norms impinge upon and shape our agency, but it is a negotiation and not a one-way street.

However, there is much more to our social engagements and agency than the ability to either enact or to criticize current norms and practices. In addition to being critical selves we are also—in an important sense—creators of ourselves. Working through and with our current social roles we forge new projects and engage new commitments with new (to us) norms and values.[1] Sometimes our decisions are transformative; sometimes they usher in entirely new (to us) kinds of norms and values. How are these features of our social agency compatible with externalism and the artisanal model? Aren't they better accommodated by internalism and an internalist explanation of the source of social role normativity? After all, for the internalist the normativity of our social roles originates in the agent, in their rational preferences or self-legislation, and these attitudes seem to be closely related to the idea of *self*-creation. The internalist seems to be well on the way to expanding on social role normativity in the right directions, namely toward novelty, personal meaning, and commitment. In contrast, the externalist, who locates the source of social role normativity in simply occupying a social position, seems to lack the resources to explain how it is possible for us to be normative self-creators. By normative self-creation I mean being responsive to norms that are new to us; a student becoming a philosopher or a person becoming a mother. We are sometimes innovative and sometimes transformed by the roles and norms that we acquire. We shape our lives and social agency; we are not simply shaped by their existing normative contours.

Despite the initial attractiveness of an internalist perspective on self-creation, I will argue that the externalist artisanal model—in fact—has better resources to explain self-creation than does internalism. I argue that Afunction externalism provides a solution to the paradox of self-creation, that is, the idea that self-creation is a process guided by values that we do not yet possess, and internalism lacks the resources to disarm the paradox.[2] The fact

---

[1] There is a distinction between self-creation as forging new projects with already existing but new to the agent norms and self-creation as creating entirely new social roles with entirely new norms. This chapter is focused on the first topic. The creation of entirely new social roles with new norms raises complex causal and normative questions that are not within the purview of this book.
[2] I argue here that neither Kantian internalism nor Humean internalism has an adequate response to the paradox of self-creation. This leaves out Hegelian internalism, but on this issue it would be subject to the same line of criticism as Kantian internalism.

that externalism can give a coherent explanation of self-creation and internalism seems to be unable to do so provides another important consideration that favors externalism. After all, normative self-creation is one of the phenomena to be explained in an account of social role normativity. But, even more important, the discussion of how externalism and the artisanal model can address and unravel the paradox of self-creation allows us to see them as having the conceptual resources required to explain a meaningful human life with projects that require normative self-creation.

The paradox of self-creation begins with the idea that self-creation is a process guided by values that we do not yet possess.[3] How is that possible? If we do not already possess the norms, how can we be guided by them? But alternatively, if we do already possess the values, then there is no creation involved because we already endorse or are responsive to the norms in question. This is the paradox of self-creation, and it poses an important challenge for any theory of social role normativity and any account of social norm acquisition. I argue in what follows that externalism about social norms provides the materials to resolve the paradox of self-creation and that internalism lacks those resources. I argue further that the most detailed and persuasive internalist attempt to address the paradox of self-creation, developed by Agnes Callard, is seriously flawed. Since self-creation is a widespread and significant human experience and the paradox of self-creation threatens our ability to explain it, the plausibility of externalism is enhanced by its ability to resolve the paradox.

Notice that self-creation differs importantly from mere self-development. Self-development refers to a process by which a person's existing norms, reasons, and goods become developed, enriched, or expanded in new directions. Always a bookish person, I learn a new language so that I can read more and different books.

---

[3] My description of the paradox of self-creation is much indebted to the discussion in Callard's *Aspiration*.

Athletic by nature, I decide to take up a new sport—rowing or skiing—in midlife. Gregarious and outgoing, I decide to inaugurate a new holiday party tradition. And so on. In these cases, my decisions are squarely planted in my existing norms and reasons for acting. Unlike self-creation, self-development does not entail the creation of a new normative self. And it avoids the paradox that threatens self-creation.

To get clearer about the phenomenon of self-creation, let's consider two examples. I call them "bait and switch" and "transformation." These examples will serve to illustrate what genuine self-creation looks like.

### Bait and Switch: From the Examined Life to Success on Wall Street

The Future of the Department Committee at UNH was tasked with pulling together a vision for the future of the Philosophy Department. Our webpage opens:

### Explore the Department of Philosophy

> UNH philosophy majors acquire the ability to think systematically and imaginatively about fundamental and enduring issues such as morality, justice, happiness, beauty, gender, race, nature, artificial intelligence, space, time, and the meaning of life and death. Our internationally renowned professors emphasize discussion, debate, and writing in our courses. Wrestling with the "big questions" from diverse and global perspectives will prepare you exceptionally well for a variety of fulfilling careers. A lively and nurturing community personally invested in the success of our high achieving students, we take pride in watching our graduates excel in top law and graduate schools, innovative

social justice programs, and various positions from Wall Street to Silicon Valley and beyond that seek hard workers who can think rigorously and communicate clearly.

Notice the dual focus in this statement. On the one hand, philosophy students address the big questions, "such as morality, justice, happiness, beauty, gender, race, nature, artificial intelligence, space, time, and the meaning of life and death." But, on the other hand, we dangle the prospect of "top law and graduate schools, innovative social justice programs, and various positions from Wall Street to Silicon Valley and beyond." Elsewhere, we publicize the lifetime earnings prospects, top performance on LSATs, and other markers of financial and professional success that correlate with an undergraduate major in philosophy.

My department's statement is typical with its dual focus on the intrinsic value of considering philosophical issues, methods, and texts, and the financial and professional benefits of studying philosophy. Sometimes we justify our advertisement of the financial and professional benefits of philosophy as helping students justify the study of philosophy to their parents. A certain unease with too much emphasis on the practical payoff of studying philosophy emerged in our discussions. And the basic reason for the unease is that none of us really think that our students should study philosophy to attain financial and professional success. If they do so, they have missed the boat. Rather than pave the way to realizing values a student in our culture might already have, we offer students an introduction to another set of norms. Our job is to help them to create themselves as beings who value thinking, reflection, and reasoning above all. In this way, mention of Wall Street, law school, and the like really is a form of bait and switch. If students leave us contented that taking logic helped with law boards as promised, they have not become philosophers, and we have failed as teachers of philosophy.

Students who change their values during the educational process from the practical goals of career and a sound financial future to the values of thinking, reflecting, and reasoning have undergone the process of self-creation in the sense I am using the term here. They have replaced one set of values or goods with another, becoming a new normative self. This is the real goal of a philosophical education, even though it may also serve more practical goods. Recall that Socrates was charged with corrupting the youth for challenging them in dialogue about their current conventional values and urging them to adopt new ones. He was challenging them to create themselves anew: to engage in normative self-creation rather than become schooled in the virtues of the Athenian elites. No wonder things went badly for him.

## Transformation: Becoming a Mother

A prime example in philosophical discussions of transformative experiences is becoming a mother, where that is sometimes described in relation to a choice at a moment, and sometimes as a process that unfolds over time. In "What You Can't Expect When You Are Expecting," L. A. Paul develops the idea that choosing to become a mother (or choosing not to become a mother) cannot be a rational decision because the values (or preferences) we have when we make the decision are not the values (or preferences) that we will come to have as mothers. So, we cannot use the former to weigh the latter; our current preferences are irrelevant to the preferences we will come to have. Having a child is what Paul calls "a transformative experience"; it is an experience that transforms a person's values (or preferences). There is a mismatch and a break between the conditions of our choice—who we are and what we want when we choose—and who we will be, and what we will want, after we become a parent. No rational choice is possible under these conditions. So, what to do? According to Paul we *can* make a rational second-order decision to either be the kind of person who wants new experiences (like a child!) or we might decide that we are not experientially adventurous (*Transformative Experience*, 122–123). But given the conceptual framework of decision theory, Paul argues, deciding to have a child, or deciding not to have a child—in itself—is not a possible rational decision.

Notice that Paul's framework of decision theory is conceptually related to Humean internalism, as I described it in Chapter 2. Rational decision making is tied to an evaluation of our current preferences, just as the Humean looks to our rational preferences to ground social role normativity. Recall that Bicchieri employs the idea of conditional social preferences to explain social norms. Our social preferences are conditioned by beliefs that we have about what others will do and how others will react to what we do. But, if Paul is right, then transformative decisions like becoming a mother cannot be based on rational preferences, because we lack the values at present that ground our future preferences. This Humean perspective lacks the resources to explain how major life decisions can be both transformative of our values and rational. But we all do in fact make major, transformative decisions, and it seems unsatisfactory that they turn out to be—in principle—inexplicable leaps of faith. Perhaps some of our major, transformative decisions *are* like leaps of faith; but Paul's argument is that they all must be. And, unless you are Kierkegaard, this is an unhappy result.

Alternatively, following Callard, we could take a different perspective on major decisions like deciding to be a mother or deciding not to be a mother. Rather than analyze a (possibly fictitious) moment of choice or decision, we could consider the temporally extended process or path of becoming a mother. This would bring the example of becoming a mother more in line with the example of becoming a philosopher. In both cases there is an extended period of reflection and activity during which the agent comes to respond to a new set of norms, ones that they did not appreciate at the beginning of the process. A student who becomes a philosopher comes to value reflection and reasoning in a way that she did not do before; a young woman who becomes a mother comes to value stability and care in ways that she did not before. Self-creation refers primarily to this normative process; it is the temporally extended creation of a self with new values, who is responsive to a new set of norms.

I think that Callard's description of the decision to become a mother as a process involving radical normative innovation may be more accurate to the experience of many mothers than Paul's description of a choice being made at a point in time to become a mother (which cannot be rational because it would require us to have values and preferences we don't have if we are not mothers). However, both scenarios occur, and it is important to see that the paradox of self-creation cannot be resolved by employing one description or the other or by replacing Paul's moment of decision with Callard's temporally extended process. The paradox of self-creation arises with both descriptions, and it just isn't possible to redescribe the examples to avoid the paradox.

## The Paradox of Self-Creation

Callard's recasting of a decisive moment of transformation into the temporally extended process of self-creation does not iron out all the conceptual kinks. Indeed, the change in focus from the moment of choice, or leap of faith, to a developmental process allows for a new difficulty to emerge. Consider Callard's description of the paradox of self-creation:

> If the value I engender in myself follows rationally from values I already have, then I do not do any creating. For in this case my "new" self was already contained in my old self. But if the new feature is rationally unconnected to my earlier values, its advent in my life cannot be my own doing. In this case, the self I end up with may be new, but it is not the product of my own agency. (104)

If the "self" part of self-creation is satisfied, then the creation part is not. Or if the creation part of self-creation is satisfied, then the "self" part is not. This is the paradox of self-creation.

In response to this paradox Callard invokes the idea of proleptic reasons that bridge the gap between old and new selves without entirely closing it. The idea of a proleptic reason satisfies the continuity requirement, as the agent already has it; but the reason or value is proleptic, meaning that it is a reason only prospectively, not for me but only for the person I aspire to become. Merriam Webster defines "prolepsis" as "the representation or assumption of a future act or development as if presently existing or accomplished." According to this definition, a proleptic reason is the representation of a future reason or value as if you already have it. But in what way is it, or can it be, a reason for you right now? It is a future reason, a reason for your future self and not for your present self.

Life-changing activities and choices are rational, not given who we are and our current set of values but guided by the goods that we aspire to fully appreciate and values we aspire to have once we become a normatively transformed person. The proleptic reason response to the paradox of self-creation appeals to teleology in two places. It explains our present choices and activities as directed toward becoming the kind of person whose actions would be guided by new goals or ends. We don't currently value them, but we want to become the person who would. Hence, a student's activities—reading, seeking out professors, attending class—are directed not only by her current values to achieve existing goals, but also by a proleptic reason, namely an appreciation of philosophical goods that she, at present, only glimpses darkly—if at all. Her studies are an act of self-creation; she becomes who she aspires to be. Similarly, a mother-to-be engages in activities that are directed toward being a person who fully appreciates maternal goods, like unconditional love or personal stability. The mother reads and thinks about them prospectively, even if she does not—as yet—grasp them fully.

Callard's discussion of what a proleptic reason is and how it can guide action situates her theory of aspiration or self-creation in the Kantian, internalist camp. Citing Korsgaard, Callard describes a guidance condition on rational activity: "Christine Korsgaard has expressed this in terms of what we might call a 'guidance condition' on rational agency: 'A person acts rationally . . . only when her action is the expression of her own mental activity. . . (118).'"[4]

Callard agrees with Korsgaard that for a reason to be action guiding it must originate in the agent's mental activity. The reason must be present to the agent or internal to the agent. Applied to the paradox of self-creation, the guidance condition requires that "in order to understand aspiration as the aspirant's own work, we need to be able to understand it as coming *from her*" (118).

Callard thinks that proleptic reasons can fill the gap between the self and who the self aspires to become. But how could a proleptic reason satisfy the guidance condition? How could a proleptic reason be action guiding and "mentally present" at the time of action? Callard introduces the idea of normative dependence to explain how proleptic reasons could be action guiding as required by the guidance condition: "We can now describe this inchoateness as a matter of normative dependence: her grasp of the reason is normatively grounded in the grasp she will have once she becomes the person she's trying to be" (121).

It is unclear to me how proleptic reasons satisfy Korsgaard's guidance condition even interpreted in terms of normative dependence. How can a reason that a student currently has to read a difficult book (to get a good grade and get into a top law school) be normatively grounded in the proleptic reason that she will have once she becomes the person she is trying to become? The mental state corresponding to "the grasp of the reason she will have once she becomes the person she is trying to be" as a mental state does not actually exist as a reason to normatively ground her current

---

[4] Ibid, 118.

inchoate understanding. The proleptic reason is *not* "mentally present to her at the time of action." Hence the proleptic reason cannot satisfy the guidance condition.

Callard's solution to the paradox of self-creation relies upon the notion of proleptic reasons; these are reasons for our temporally extended choices and activities that we will fully grasp only after we have become the new normative self that we have created. If the notion of a proleptic reason cannot satisfy the guidance condition, then Callard has not succeeded in solving the paradox of self-creation in terms that are acceptable to an internalist like Korsgaard who thinks of values and norms as grounded in the self and legislated by the self. How can you self-legislate a norm or engage a value that will only bind your future self or that is only a value for your future self? Neither the future self nor the future self's values exist. On what then does the proleptic reason normatively depend?

As we have just seen, explaining transformative experiences and self-creation is problematic for internalists in the context of social role normativity. We have only considered two types of internalism, of course, but they are suggestive of an underlying problem. If the source of normativity is the self, either with its current preferences or through a session of self-legislation, then it is difficult to explain how our norms are structured in a complex teleological fashion. But the resolution of the paradox of self-creation requires just this. I think that Afunction externalism has conceptual resources to explain just how this happens. As it turns out, and despite our initial hunches, Afunction externalism is better able to explain self-creation than its internalist rivals.

## The Paradox of Self-Creation Revisited

Let's go back to the paradox of self-creation. How does an individual transcend their current set of norms to embrace truly novel (to them) values? I have suggested that two internalist approaches face serious conceptual problems. But what does Afunction externalism have to offer? In brief, the artisanal model offers a location for the goods and norms that are the objects of aspiration for the apprentice. The apprentice wants to become a certain kind of person with a set of norms and values, to which they will be responsive. The apprentice's activities and decisions are directed toward those individuals who model activities, attitudes, norms. The apprentice wants to become an expert. This is an act of self-creation in the sense that the apprentice lacks, but the expert they want to become has a grasp of, the normative tool set that makes up expertise. The apprentice wants to become an expert, even though the apprentice does not grasp or fully grasp what that means. The normative standard, at which the apprentice aims, is exemplified by role models—real people, characters in literature, and the like. The normative standard is not a nonexistent mental entity in the agent. It is embodied out there in the world in the person of the expert. The goal of the teleological process is right there in front of the classroom, or in the room next door feeding the baby. Or perhaps in front of the classroom feeding the baby.

The Afunction account of self-creation turns our focus away from the mind and its current and future contents, and toward agental concepts like imitation, habituation, and practice. The concept of imitation presupposes that there exist individuals—experts—from whom we can and do learn both how to act, and why to act in those ways. The ideas of practice and habituation point to the process of development from apprentice to expert, a blend of gradually increasing levels of know-how and know-why. At some point the second stage goal is met; the apprentice has become an expert, who is an individual with both know-how and know-why—with teachable expertise.

The Afunction externalist explanation of social role normativity has resources for explaining self-creation that skirts the paradox of self-creation. It allows us to locate a good or goal that is the immediate end of the person's actions while at the same time allowing that the full normative content of the goal might be initially opaque to the individual. Using the apprentice model, we can see that one can have a reason for striving to become an x, from one's current position, even when one doesn't know what the reasons for being an x are for the person who is an x. The first-year student might, for example, admire Professor Smith and want to be like them, even if they do not know exactly what that means or precisely what Professor Smith's values are. You want to be like a person, an expert or a role model, and you imitate them without exactly knowing what that person values or why. You have a goal *de re* (to be like Professor Smith) but not *de dicto* (to be a philosopher, someone who values reason, the world of ideas, and critical thinking).[5] However, in accomplishing your goal *de re* and becoming like Professor Smith, you will be creating yourself with a new set of norms and values. The apprentice learning model explains how that occurs using the notions of imitation, practice, and habituation.

Similarly, one might want to be like one's mother, or a friend who has a child, without explicitly knowing what maternal norms are or without sharing their maternal norms. In this case you would want to be like a person, a role model, without exactly knowing what that person values or why. Your aspirations have a goal (be like your mother) without you being able to say what your mother values. You have a goal *de re* (be like your mother) but not *de dicto* (be a mother—someone who values love, care, and stability). However, in accomplishing your goal *de re* and becoming like your mother, you will be creating yourself with a new set of norms and values.

In the Afunction explanation of self-creation, the social role norms are initially external to the self-creator. The double teleology works as follows. First, one aspires to be like a certain individual (Professor Smith, your mother) and then, through imitation, practice, and habituation, one learns to respond to the appropriate

---

[5] Mark Okrent suggested using the distinction between having a goal *de re* and having a goal *de dicto* to explain the nested teleology of self-creation.

values and norms in the way in which an individual in that social position does (philosophical norms, maternal norms). The norms in question are those that constitute expertise and technique as appropriate to the type of social role in question. Externalism concerning the source of social role normativity and the artisanal model have conceptual resources that allow us to unravel the paradox of self-creation. Normative self-creation is an important component of a meaningful human life; it is fair to say that it is an important component of most of our lives.

## Conclusion

In Chapters 5 and 6 I have addressed a deep and persistent intuition about externalist approaches to social role normativity, which is that they model our social agency as if we were robots programmed by external forces to behave in conventional ways, and to automatically conform to social role norms. Heidegger's term *das Man* comes to mind with its depressing connotations of inevitable social conformity and herd mentality.[6] The artisanal model for social role normativity has proven useful in countering that mistaken intuition about an externalist approach to the origin of social role normativity. The artisanal model makes room for familiar forms of social norm criticism, and for normative self-creation and personal commitment to meaningful activities. Indeed, thinking about social role norms on the model of artisanal norms allows us to see the norms in terms of technique and expertise, and as empowering us rather than as simply imprisoning us.

These observations raise several questions about the ways in which social roles fit into the larger social fabric, because it might

---

[6] For a discussion of several interpretations of Heidegger's concept of *das Man* relevant to the topics in this chapter, see "Interpreting Heidegger on *Das Man*" in Dreyfus, *Background Practices*.

be the case that, taken in isolation, a particular social role is a way of realizing a technique to do or to make something or to be a kind of person. It might be that the related expertise is empowering in the ways just described. But social roles don't exist in isolation, and they are often arranged in hierarchical patterns of domination and subordination—for example, the chef and the line cook, the teacher and the student, the man and the woman. On the one hand, we might agree that each role is potentially equally empowering viewed in isolation; each is equally realized by a set of techniques, responsiveness to which constitutes expertise in the individual. And experts are responsive to normatively evaluable techniques to do or make things that those lacking expertise are not responsive to. But it just seems dead obvious that these roles are differentially empowering due to the hierarchical relations among social roles. The same is even more clearly true of social roles that are most deeply embedded in the hierarchical and oppressive structure of our social world—like gender and race.

In the next chapter we consider the relationships among social roles that are suggested by the artisanal model. After all, artisans ply their trades with each other, which requires social coordination both within a single trade and among different trades. And the same can be said about other social roles, such as familial roles. In many social systems, like the workplace or the family, roles are hierarchically organized. Are all hierarchically organized systems also oppressive? How does the artisanal model depict the possible relationships among social roles in the larger social fabric?

# 7
# The Artisanal Model and Social Hierarchy

As I mentioned in Chapter 1, my initial inspiration for this book came from thinking about gendered social roles and wondering about the source of their normativity. I was struck by the force, number, and complexity of gendered social norms and their centrality in our lives. It was also striking the extent to which, like racialized social roles, they are firmly enmeshed in oppressive, hierarchical relations. It is time to come full circle and to see the implications of the artisanal model for the hierarchical and oppressive relations among social positions and social roles. In this chapter I develop two points. First, I show how the artisanal model helps to explain the oppressive and hierarchical structure of some social positions and roles, including contemporary gendered or racialized social roles. Second, I argue that oppressive and hierarchical relations are not a necessary feature of the artisanal model and that the model also suggests the possibility of nonhierarchical and nonoppressive relations among social roles. Using the artisanal model, we can imagine a social world with techniques for being human that are not enmeshed in oppressive, hierarchical relations. We can imagine an artisanal work space that is organized horizontally rather than vertically.

Social roles are sources of normativity that also provide ways of coordinating our social lives. These two features of social roles are not independent of one another; it is as sources of normativity that social roles function to coordinate our social agency. For example, gendered social roles coordinate many types of behavior

*Social Goodness.* Charlotte Witt, Oxford University Press. © Oxford University Press 2023.
DOI: 10.1093/oso/9780197574799.003.0007

normatively—in the family, in the workplace, in the bar after work. Given one's gender, there are things one ought to do and things one ought not to do in a certain context, and these norms help to coordinate our behavior. The coordinating work is often invisible and becomes apparent only when a norm is not observed or is breached. The example of gender raises an important question about the nature of the coordinating relationship among social roles on the artisanal model, because gender roles often coordinate social behavior in an oppressive and hierarchical fashion. And in some cultural contexts, the same can be said of racialized social roles.

What does the artisanal model tell us about the character of the relationships among social positions and social roles? How does the coordination of social positions and social roles work? Does the coordination of social positions and roles require a hierarchical relationship among the positions and the roles? And are the hierarchical relations always oppressive? Finally, does the artisanal model suggest novel ways of coordinating social positions and social roles?

Before tackling these questions, a brief review is in order. The dialectic of this book opens in Chapter 1 with a discussion of the central question of this book, namely what is the source of social role normativity. Chapter 2 continues with an argument for normative externalism concerning the source of social role normativity. The source of normativity is the social role, and the reason that an individual is responsive to and evaluable under a norm is that they occupy the relevant social position. This line of thought continues with the proposal in Chapter 3 that we understand normative externalism using the artisanal model for social roles. The artisanal model allows us to see how individuals can stand under norms simply by virtue of their identity or, in other words, because of their social position occupancy. A carpenter ought to use a level because they are a carpenter. Artisanal techniques, normatively assessable ways of doing things or making things, provide a useful model for all social roles, which are also ways of doing and making things that are normatively assessable. A mother ought to care for her children because she is a mother. Chapter 4 developed the ontology and the explanatory resources of the artisanal model to argue that it requires a nonindividualist social ontology. The artisanal model requires a richer ontology than methodological individualism can provide, and the model incorporates explanatory resources that exceed the resources of methodological individualism. Chapters 5 and 6 reverse direction and turn our attention to the individual agent, and the way in which the individual's critical and creative powers are developed, retained, and even enhanced according to the artisanal model. An externalist account of the source of social role normativity understood on the artisanal model enables criticism by individuals of the norms to which they are responsive. The model also allows for a coherent and nonparadoxical explanation of normative self-creation, which is an important element in our projects and meaningful engagements.

In this chapter the dialectical pendulum swings back again to the larger social world and the relationship among positions and roles in the social fabric. Earlier chapters have noted the cultural, historical, and material embeddedness of social positions and roles according to the artisanal model. Indeed, it is a strength of the artisanal model that it incorporates and clearly displays these forms of the situatedness of social normativity. The central focus in this chapter is on the relationship among social roles, and the implications of these relationships for the individuals who stand under them. But let's begin with a review of the situatedness of social roles.

## The Situatedness of Social Roles

One of the strengths of the artisanal model is the picture it paints of social roles as deeply embedded in cultural, historical, and material contexts. Social positions and roles, normatively inflected ways of doing things, are always local; they are situated in a particular culture, in a set of material conditions, and at a particular historical moment. The artisanal model captures the contextual character of social role norms in the notion of local standards of excellence that do not yield to a purely instrumental explanation. Think about all the ways in which artisanal goals are achieved; think about all the local standards of excellence and local craft traditions. For example, consider all the different dining and culinary traditions that have local norms and standards of excellence. Like craft traditions, social role norms express local standards of excellence in relation to the social positions available in a culture. The situatedness of social roles displayed by the artisanal model captures an important dimension of social roles, which is that they are what you ought to do around here if you occupy a certain social position. The locality of artisanal norms provides a way of articulating the locality of social role norms. This is particularly relevant in relation to social roles like race and gender, where theorists note variability across social contexts, but it also applies to social roles more broadly. In other words, the obvious variability in gendered or racialized social roles is not peculiar to them but is shared by many other social roles. Normative variability is a central feature of the artisanal model, and it usefully captures and expresses the variability of social role norms.

Another important aspect of the artisanal model concerns the embeddedness of social roles in the material world. By the material world I don't primarily mean the world of atoms and void, but rather the world of materials—material resources, material availability, or abundance/scarcity and the like. Artisans require materials of various kinds to develop and apply their techniques and so do individuals who occupy various social positions. What one ought to do (given who you are) is dependent upon the material organization of the world in your neighborhood, and the same is true concerning your ability to do what you ought to do given the social position(s) you occupy. Our engagement with social role norms is grounded in the material affordances in our neighborhood.

The norms a potter is responsive to and evaluable under presuppose certain material conditions, as does the potter's ability to respond to the norms. Both the norms a mother is responsive to and evaluable under and the possibility of their fulfillment presuppose material resources, and these vary by location. Moreover, which social roles exist in a social setting, and how social roles relate to one another, are also influenced by the local material conditions. For example, in Iceland a technique for building houses with turf roofs developed, reflecting locally available building materials and local conditions. In these ways the artisanal model for social role normativity displays the social and material situatedness of social role norms. But what about the relationships among the social roles within a given social context?

Before turning to that question, it is important to note that all three facets of the situatedness of social positions and roles—cultural, historical, and material—condition the relationships among social roles. And a full discussion of the relationships among social positions and roles would develop this point in some detail. In what follows, to keep the discussion manageable, I will bracket further discussion of the situatedness of social roles even though it conditions the possible relations among social positions and roles.

## Social Roles and Social Coordination

The artisanal model exemplifies two kinds of relationships among social roles, and these are useful to distinguish. First, the artisanal model depicts various artisanal activities as being what they are only in relation to other artisanal activities. Brick makers have the function they have in relation to builders who use bricks to build houses and so on. Similarly, social roles function in systems of internally related roles, and not as independent actions or activities that are woven together only externally. For example, familial and workplace social roles are defined in relation to one another and not simply juxtaposed externally. You cannot say what a mother is without reference to other family members and who they are; you cannot be a mother without standing in a particular relation to other family members. Social roles are never a one-off; they always are ontologically related to other social roles. For this reason, it is useful to think of a social role system, or multiple systems, at varying levels of complexity.

Second, according to our model, the normative character of artisanal techniques is secured by relationship to other artisanal techniques. Brick making techniques are normatively evaluable ways of making bricks, and the techniques are good or bad in relation to how houses are built around here. The same applies to other social roles. Being a mother is a social role that is composed of normatively evaluable ways of being maternal around here, and the value of these techniques is calibrated in relation to others in related social roles (e.g., being paternal), whose techniques are normatively evaluable in relation to them. In sum, social roles are relational both ontologically and normatively.

However, there is even more structure to the relationships among social roles than I have indicated until now. In addition to the relational character of social roles ontologically and normatively, the artisanal model depicts social roles as ordered in a holistic fashion. The artisanal model is holistic because the value of a particular artisanal activity is calibrated in relation to the whole to which it contributes. The line cook's activities are valued in relation to the whole meal; and the character of the meal (and, indeed, the entire menu) is determined by the chef. To appreciate what the line cook is doing, what norms they are responsive to, you need to understand it in relation to the production of the whole meal. And to appreciate the meal you need to understand the norms governing the menu, to which the chef is responsive when composing it. The skills of the line cook and the chef are calibrated in relation to a larger whole. The character of the evaluation is holistic, and the normatively assessable techniques are such in relation to the larger activity or practice of which they are a part and to which they contribute. What is true within a given artisanal practice holds between them when they "fall under a single power" (*EN*, I, 1 1094a8). In Aristotle's example, the "horsey" arts (bridle making, training of rider and horse) are what they are in relation to the equestrian art. So, the various equestrian goals or goods, and hence the normative character of the ingredient social roles, are ordered teleologically in terms of the overall goal or good. The artisanal model depicts social roles as holistic both ontologically and normatively.

The holism of the artisanal model provides resources to address problematic examples of social roles, like being a thief. On the artisanal model a skilled thief is responsive to and evaluable under the techniques that are normatively assessable ways of performing the function of a thief. There are skilled thieves and unskilled thieves. Even though the artisanal model can make sense of this distinction, it seems paradoxical or at least unsatisfactory to hold that there are norms a thief ought to follow and ways they ought to do things in the same sense that there are things a mother ought to do and ways she ought to do them. If we just consider social roles one by one, we are left with the idea that the artisanal model actually does not capture or express social normativity adequately, since it seems to be unable to differentiate between techniques for being a thief and techniques for being a mother. How can the artisanal model handle this difference?

To see how the artisanal model can handle examples like the thief it is helpful to recall that social roles are ontologically and normatively interrelated in a holistic system. There is a straightforward sense in which a thief might be skilled at their "job," but the role itself is not a cohesive part of the social system. Just at the level of the social system, without leaving the bounds of social norms and without invoking ethical or political principles, we can say that thieves "ought not" perform their function irrespective of whether they do so skillfully or not.

The example of the excellent or skilled enslaver is similar to the skillful thief in some respects. As with the example of the thief it is important to recall that the goodness in question is social goodness or goodness in relation to a social system and not ethical goodness.

Unlike the social role of thief, however, the social role of enslaver (for example, in the US) was deeply intertwined with other roles both ontologically and normatively, and securely tethered to local traditions. The role of enslaver seems to have been embedded in the social fabric rather than a flaw or a rip in it. The enslaver, unlike the thief, does not seem to be intrinsically at odds with other social positions their social world and so we can't generate a criticism of the social role in these terms.

Of course, we can criticize the social role of enslaver from an external ethical or political perspective. But we cannot seem to say, as we could with the thief, that the holistic ontology and normativity of social roles just in themselves provide grounds to say that the enslaver ought not perform their function irrespective of whether they do so skillfully or not. Of course it is open to us to argue that the social role of enslaver is not a coherent part of the social system and for that reason, like the thief, the enslaver is neither socially good nor ethically good.

The holism of the artisanal model grounds the normative coordination of social roles. It is because artisanal activity forms systems that are interconnected ontologically and normatively that they can function to coordinate behavior. And the same is true of social roles in general. It is because they form systems (e.g., family systems, workplace systems) and are interconnected both ontologically and normatively that they can perform their coordination function. Does the artisanal model require further that the coordinating relationship among social positions and social roles is of a particular kind? Is a hierarchical relationship among social positions and social roles required for their coordination?

## Social Roles and Social Hierarchy

There are, of course, many kinds of social hierarchies and many ways to explain them. For our purposes, to say that the relationship between social positions and roles is hierarchical is to ascribe a normative ordering to the relationship. A normative ordering obtains when the occupant of one position, the boss, can tell the occupant of another position, the worker, what they ought to do, how they ought to do it, and whether they have done it well, but not vice versa. When I talk about hierarchies in what follows, I will be talking about normative hierarchies. On the artisanal model the three aspects of normative hierarchies can come apart. Maybe the foreman, to do their job well, ought to tell the carpenter what needs to be made, but not how to do it or whether it has been done well. Those judgments are made by the carpenter and their fellow artisans and not by the foreman. The artisanal model allows for, indeed invites, this kind of complex normative situation.

I borrow from feminist theory the idea that a normative hierarchy is oppressive if the occupant of one social position systematically subordinates the occupant of another social position due to the hierarchical relationship among the social positions they occupy. The kind of oppression or subordination at issue in relation to normative hierarchy is normative subordination or oppression. Normative subordination happens in many ways. One example, mentioned above, happens when a foreman tells the skilled carpenter not only what to make but also how to make it and whether it has been made well. When I talk about subordination or oppression in what follows, I will be talking about normative subordination or oppression. I follow feminist theorists like Iris Marion Young in holding that oppression does not refer primarily to a relationship between two individuals, but rather to the relationship between social positions and social roles. Normative oppression is one form that structural oppression can take.

Social positions and roles can be related nonhierarchically (horizontally), hierarchically (vertically), and hierarchically in an oppressive fashion. Let us begin with a discussion of hierarchical relations among social positions and social roles. Two features of the artisanal model are particularly relevant to an assessment of its hierarchical tendencies. The first feature is the artisanal learning model or the way in which techniques are transmitted from expert to apprentice. The second feature is the holistic character of the model: the way that social positions are coordinated to get the job done. Must they always be coordinated in a hierarchical fashion?

Skills and expertise flow from expert to novice in the artisanal model. The novice-expert relationship is central to the transmission (and development) of artisanal technique. And the transmission of technique is hierarchical: it flows in one direction, from expert to apprentice. It is not a two-way street between equal partners, because in relation to the transmission of artisanal technique, experts and novices are not equal partners. The acquisition of technique is both a hierarchical process and a necessary feature of the artisanal model. Recall that for the Aristotelian, habituation—or the process by which we become experts—is part of what it is to be an expert. Expertise is the endpoint of a process; it is not a divine gift or momentary inspiration. And the same is true of social roles on the artisanal model. So, on the artisanal model, we can't just bracket the hierarchical transmission process by which we become experts from the expertise we gain; they are interwoven. To be an expert in x is, among other things, to have gone through an apprenticeship process as an x under the guidance of an expert (or experts). We cannot isolate the hierarchical process by which we become responsive to a social role from our subsequent responsiveness to that role. The ability to respond to the relevant social norms just is the result of a process of habituation, imitation, and guided practice. This feature of the model is intrinsically hierarchical.

It might be useful to recall at this point, as I argued in Chapters 5 and 6, that the artisanal model, despite the hierarchical character of the apprenticeship process, leaves room for, and even empowers, norm criticism, and norm creativity. So, although the acquisition of expertise is an intrinsically hierarchical process on the artisanal model, it does not follow that our responsiveness to social role norms is as well. There is a wide range of possible responses to the social role norms an individual is responsive to and evaluable under. Indeed, one type of responsiveness to a social norm is to criticize or reject it. Moreover, while the process of learning to be an expert requires a hierarchical relationship between social positions and roles, the fact that part of what it is to be an expert involves the capacity to criticize the relevant norms also implies that the result of the process of apprenticeship is not one of subordination or oppression of the student to their teacher. Of course, the relationship could be both hierarchical and oppressive; the point is that it need not be. The hierarchical relationship between expert and apprentice during the transmission process can give way to a normatively egalitarian relationship between peers. Indeed, in many instances, the transmission process that does not end this way is arguably a failure.

Does social role holism require a hierarchical organization? Though the artisanal model is holistic, which is facilitated by coordination among social positions and social roles, these need not be coordinated in a hierarchical fashion. In the artisanal context the determination of what is to be done and how, and whether it has been done well, is often determined by the artisans themselves, either singly or as a group. It is part of artisanal technique to be able to determine the order of tasks, the manner of completing them, and whether they have been done well. Hence, we should distinguish between the observation that many artisanal fields are, in fact, organized hierarchically and the idea that this way of organizing them is an inherent feature of the model. On the contrary, the artisanal model suggests the possibility of nonhierarchical, horizontal coordination of social positions and social roles. Because oppressive relations among social positions and roles presuppose hierarchy, and the model suggests the possibility of nonhierarchical relations, it also allows for nonoppressive relations. The bridle maker doesn't tell the saddle maker what to do or how to do it or whether what has been done has been done well or badly. Nor does the saddle maker tell the bridle maker what to do and how to do it. Nonetheless, their creative activities are often normatively coordinated. The same is true of other social roles; many of them are—in fact—organized hierarchically (familial roles, professional roles) but the coordination function of social roles does not require a hierarchical organization of social positions and social roles. For example, faculty governance at some colleges and universities in the United States assumes that faculty are best positioned to determine what to teach, how to teach, and whether teaching has been done well. And there are many other kinds of labor co-ops or unions that are structured in a nonhierarchical fashion. Since subordination presupposes hierarchical relations among social positions and social roles, some parts of the social world are structured in a nonhierarchical and nonoppressive fashion.

The artisanal model suggests that we distinguish among hierarchies that are embedded in the transmission of technique and the creation of expertise (transmission hierarchies), and those that are the result of coordination efforts (coordination hierarchies). As I have already noted, transmission hierarchies are a fixed feature of the artisanal model. But for individual social agents they are often part of a process that is also transitory, empowering, and a source of social meaning. Coordination hierarchies are not a fixed feature of the artisanal model, but they are a frequent means of coordinating social agency. Just as it is not a necessary feature of a building site that the various trades and workers be organized hierarchically, but they often are, so too it is not a necessary feature of the nuclear family that it be organized hierarchically around gender roles, but it often is.

I have been arguing that the artisanal model is not intrinsically hierarchical, with the sole exception of the process of transmission of artisanal techniques. The transmission process is both hierarchical and conservative as standing techniques are passed on by experts to novices. This aspect of the model helps to explain both the persistence of social role norms and their resistance to change. But some social roles, like gender roles and racialized roles, appear to be firmly bound up in hierarchical relations in a manner that is not captured by the hierarchical feature of the artisanal model, namely the transmission process. The image of the apprentice watchmaker learning their trade from an expert, and then practicing it by being responsive to the norms that comprise the technique of watchmaking seems to be entirely inadequate to account for the hierarchical entanglement of social roles like gender or race in the social fabric. And thinking about them in terms of the organizational hierarchy of an artisanal workplace also seems not to quite capture the ways in which social roles like these are persistent and powerfully hierarchical and oppressive, even when there are other means of social coordination or when they don't transparently or efficiently serve a coordination function. What are the resources and limitations of the artisanal model in relation to gendered and racialized social roles or in relation to other social roles that are persistently or powerfully hierarchical?

## The Persistence of Hierarchy

We have already seen that the transmission of technique, from the expert to the novice, is hierarchical on the artisanal model; the expert and the novice are not equal partners in the process. The hierarchy is normative. The expert, in response to their social role norms, ought to tell the novice what they ought to, how they ought to do it, and whether they have done it well; in doing so the expert is doing what an expert ought to do in the situation. We noted that while the relationship between the expert and the apprentice is hierarchical, it need not be oppressive as well; the apprentice need not be subordinated or oppressed by the expert. However, the hierarchical structure of the transmission process lays a groundwork for persisting hierarchical relationships.

The transmission of artisanal technique via imitation, habituation, and guided practice tends to conserve not only individual techniques but also relations among techniques. Recall that social positions and roles are normatively and ontologically related to one another. They form systems. The process of social role learning on the artisanal model is never single or atomistic; we are always acquiring sets of interrelated norms. And if the relationship among these systems and sets of roles and positions is hierarchical then that feature will also tend to be passed on. The artisanal model explains the conservation of hierarchical social relations via the way the model explains the transmission of technique.

Because of their long tentacles, social roles like gender and race are deeply embedded in normative hierarchical systems: doctor/nurse, executive/administrative assistant, teacher/student, professor/lecturer. These examples of normative hierarchies include gendered and raced hierarchies that are interwoven in the hierarchical systems in an oppressive fashion. Normative hierarchies of gender and race are interwoven strands in a mutually reinforcing fabric. In societies like ours, gender and race snake through and strengthen hierarchical systems that are also oppressive.

I have been describing the ways in which the systematic character of social positions and roles together with the artisanal learning model support the conservation of normative hierarchies. The artisanal model has additional resources to explain the persistence of norms, namely the situatedness of social role norms. Recall that cultures and their material and historical conditions help to explain the social role norms or standards of excellence that obtain around here. The weight of local traditions is undoubtedly a significant factor in explaining the persistence of social role norms, including normative hierarchies that are oppressive or subordinating.

It is important to balance the resources of the artisanal model to explain the persistence and resistance to change of social role normativity against the resources of the model to explain norm criticism and normative self-creation. On the individual level the model provides resources to explain norm criticism and nonconformity. These are important explananda for a theory of social role normativity. And it also allows for individuals to engage in normative self-creation in a way that resolves the paradox of self-creation. It is a strength of the artisanal model that it has resources both to explain the evident persistence of normative hierarchies that are oppressive and to explain normative critique and innovation.

These two features of the artisanal model are related to one another via the notions of habituation and imitation. The transmission process of the artisanal model is conservative, as the processes of habituation, imitation, and guided practice convey techniques of being human from one generation to the next. But the transmission process is also a source of normative innovation. These very same processes—or habituation, imitation, and guided practice—develop a generalized sense of excellence that provides a vantage point from which to criticize or to change particular social role norms (or techniques for being human). These very same processes empower individuals to become social role critics and nonconformers, and to become self-creators who are able to develop new normative selves.

# Epilogue

## Social Roles and Oppression

"Cages. Consider a birdcage. If you look very closely at just one wire in the cage, you cannot see the other wires. If your conception of what is before you is determined by this myopic focus, you could look at that one wire, up and down the length of it, and be unable to see why a bird would not just fly around the wire any time it wanted to go somewhere" (12).

Marilyn Frye

"As I see it, a racial identity is a kind of know-how for navigating one's position in a racialized social space. The apt content for a racial identity, then, may be positive, affirming, and empowering, even if the racialized social position one occupies is oppressive" (Glasgow et al. 30).

Sally Haslanger

As I mentioned in the preface, I began to think about the source of social role normativity in relation to gendered social roles, and it seems fitting to return to that theme and context now. My reflections here are framed by two quotations from feminist philosophers Marilyn Frye and Sally Haslanger. Marilyn Frye's famous birdcage image is powerful in expressing how it is that we can be responsive to and evaluable under oppressive social norms without even realizing it, and that these oppressive norms form systems that are often invisible to us. In the preface I used a joke about fish in the sea to convey a similar point about the ubiquity and invisibility of social norms. Frye's image is particularly effective in expressing that point. She also captures another important insight about social norms, which is that we often have the illusion of freedom about them. Like the bird in the cage, we tend to believe that we are not, in fact, obligated or bound by social role norms, but could choose to turn around and fly away from them. But, as Frye's image depicts, that is an illusion.

But what exactly is the illusion? Perhaps I understand the illusion slightly differently from Frye. Like Frye's birdcage, the artisanal model captures and expresses the pervasive presence of social positions and social roles in our lives, and the systematic and relational character of social roles, both ontologically and normatively. And the artisanal model also illustrates those features of social roles that tend toward hierarchical and oppressive relations. These features include both the transmission of expertise and the need for organization of artisanal workplaces. But Frye's birdcage image strongly suggests in addition that social roles, singly and as systems, are simply oppressive. To be free is simply to escape the constraints of social norms altogether: to get out of the cage. Individually, they are bars in the cage that reinforce one another in a systematic fashion. Cages limit freedom; to be free, one must escape from the cage of oppressive social norms. Translating the image into words, we might conclude that social norms and social roles only limit the freedom of human agency, and that we should try to free ourselves from them.

I have argued in this book that this is only one side of the story. To see the other side, we are helped by the second quotation from Sally Haslanger concerning racial identity and racialized social spaces. Using an artisanal vocabulary, Haslanger describes racial identity as "a kind of know-how" for negotiating a racialized culture. And this know-how is, or can be, empowering. The normative content of a racialized social role, the techniques for being a racialized person (in context) are not simply oppressive and limiting, as Frye might have it, they can also be enabling and empowering. As I read her,

Haslanger adds something important to Frye's powerful image of the bird cage.[1]

The artisanal model for social role normativity depicts social roles, ways of being human, as both limiting and empowering as suggested by Haslanger. It is useful to distinguish between the social role or technique associated with a social position and the system comprised of social positions and social roles. I have argued that the artisanal model allows us to understand that the notions of technique and expertise are both limiting and empowering. Learning how to do something or to make something enlarges possibilities even as it requires responsiveness to and evaluation under the norms of the technique. The artisanal model depicts artisanal positions and roles as relational and systematic both ontologically and normatively. Hierarchical and oppressive relations among social roles are a clear possibility on the artisanal model, but we can also imagine artisanal workplaces as organized in different ways, and not all of them are hierarchical or oppressive.

Most important, just as techniques make individual artisanal expertise possible, so too techniques for being human, or social roles, make possible our individual social know-how. Haslanger's example is useful here too; our social role know-how or expertise gives us the ability to navigate social spaces successfully even when the social spaces are organized in an oppressive fashion. The artisanal image is useful for mapping the complex dialectic of empowerment and limitation, of freedom and oppression that structures our social lives and that we experience every day. Just as the artisan could not engage in their craft without technique and expertise, so too we humans, as social individuals, could not engage our lives without social role norms, without ways of being human.

---

[1] Arguably Frye's birdcage image was intended simply to illustrate our illusion of freedom from oppressive social norms as well as their systematic character. These are very important pieces of the puzzle of social norms.

Like all good images, Frye's cage is selective: it depicts important features of social norms that are oppressive; we don't grasp them clearly; we don't understand they are systematic; we are under the illusion of freedom. All that is importantly right. But it is not the whole story. Just as an artisan's freedom is circumscribed by artisanal technique and the norms to which they respond and under which they are evaluated, so too, the artisan is enabled and empowered by their expertise to be able to criticize and to innovate the standards under which they stand. And most important, this expertise in a technique is necessary to enable the artisan to perform her artisanal function, and to produce her artisanal products. Artisans and artisanal practice provide particularly rich resources for depicting the fundamental duality of all social roles; like artisanal expertise and technique, social role normativity is both limiting and empowering. Moreover, thinking of social roles as techniques for being human helps us to understand how it is that we could be responsive to and evaluable under social role norms quite independently of our attitudes toward them. In addition, the artisanal model depicts the material, historical, and cultural situatedness of social roles. Finally, the artisanal model allows us to realize that without social roles, without techniques for being human, we would not be able to engage with each other in our social world. Social roles are, quite simply, ways of being human.

# Select Bibliography

Anderson, Elizabeth. "Beyond *Homo Economicus*: New Developments in Theories of Social Norms." *Philosophy and Public Affairs*, vol. 29, no. 2, 2000, pp. 170–200.

Annas, Julia. "Practical Expertise." *Knowing How: Essays on Knowledge, Mind, and Action*, edited by John Bengson and Marc A. Moffett, Oxford, 2012, pp. 101–112.

Annas, Julia. "Virtue as a Skill." *International Journal of Philosophical Studies*, vol. 3, no. 2, 1995, pp. 227–243.

Ásta. *Categories We Live By*. Oxford, 2018.

Barnes, Jonathan. *The Complete Works of Aristotle: The Revised English Translation*. Oxford, 1984.

Barney, Rachel. "Aristotle's Argument for a Human Function." *Oxford Studies in Ancient Philosophy*, vol. 34, 2008, pp. 293–322.

Bicchieri, Cristina. *Norms in the Wild: How to Diagnose, Measure, and Change Social Norms*. Oxford, 2017.

Bicchieri, Cristina, et al. "Social Norms." *The Stanford Encyclopedia of Philosophy* (Winter 2018 Edition), edited by Edward N. Zalta. https://plato.stanford.edu/archives/win2018/entries/social-norms/.

Blackman, Reid. "Roles Ground Reasons; So Internalism Is False." *PEA Soup: Philosophy, Ethics, Academia*. http://peasoup.us/2017/01/roles-ground-reasons-internalism-false-reid-blackman/

Brandom, Robert B. *Reason in Philosophy: Animating Ideas*. Belknap, 2009.

Brennan, Geoffrey, et al. *Explaining Norms*. Oxford, 2013.

Broadie, Sarah Waterlow. *Ethics with Aristotle*. Oxford, 1994.

Callard, Agnes. *Aspiration: The Agency of Becoming*. Oxford, 2018.

Cummins, Robert. "Functional Analysis." *Journal of Philosophy*, vol. 72, 1975, pp. 741–764.

Davidson, Lacey J., and Daniel Kelly. "Minding the Gap: Bias, Soft Structures, and the Double Life of Social Norms." *Journal of Applied Philosophy*, vol. 37, 2018, pp. 190–210.

Dreyfus, Hubert. *Background Practices: Essays on the Understanding of Being*. Oxford, 2017.

Dreyfus, Hubert. *Skillful Coping: Essays on the Phenomenology of Everyday Perception and Action*. Oxford, 2017.

Epstein, Brian. *The Ant Trap: Rebuilding the Foundations of the Social Sciences*. Oxford, 2015.

Fossheim, Halvard. "Habituation as *Mimesis*." *Values and Virtues: Aristotelianism in Contemporary Ethics*, edited by Timothy Chappell, Oxford, 2006, pp. 105-117.

Friedland, Ellan. "Problems with Intellectualism." *Philosophical Studies*, vol. 165, no. 3, 2013, pp. 879-891.

Frye, Marilyn. *The Politics of Reality – Essays in Feminist Theory*. Potter/TenSpeed/Harmony/Rodale, 1983.

Glasgow, Joshua, et al. *What Is Race?: Four Philosophical Views*. Oxford, 2019.

Hardimon, Michael O. "Role Obligations." *The Journal of Philosophy*, vol. 91, no. 7, 1994, pp. 333-363.

Haslanger, Sally. "Failures of Methodological Individualism: The Materiality of Social Systems." *Journal of Social Philosophy*, vol. 53, 2022, pp. 512-534.

Haslanger, Sally. "Gender and Race: (What) Are They? (What) Do We Want Them To Be?" *Noûs*, vol. 34, no. 1, 2000, pp. 31-55.

Hufendiek, Rebekka, et al. *Social Functions in Philosophy*. Routledge, 2020.

Jenkins, Katharine. "Toward an Account of Gender Identity." *Ergo*, vol. 5, no. 27, 2018, pp. 713-744.

Korsgaard, Christine M. "Aristotle's Function Argument." *The Constitution of Agency: Essays on Practical Reason and Moral Psychology*. Oxford, 2008, pp. 129-150.

Korsgaard, Christine M. "Personal Identity and the Unity of Agency." *Personal Identity*, edited by Raymond Martin & John Baressi, Blackwell, 2003, pp. 168-183.

Korsgaard, Christine M. *The Sources of Normativity*. Cambridge, 1996.

Krohs, Ulrich, and Peter Kroes editors. *Functions in Biological and Artificial Worlds: Comparative Philosophical Perspectives*. MIT Press, 2009.

Lawson, T. *The Nature of Social Reality*. Routledge, 2009.

MacIntyre, Alasdair, *After Virtue*. University of Notre Dame, 1981.

Mallon, Ron. *The Construction of Human Kinds*. Oxford, 2016.

Mallon, Ron. "Social Construction, Social Roles and Stability." *Socializing Metaphysics: The Nature of Social Reality*, edited by Frederick F. Schmitt, Rowman & Littlefield, 2003, pp. 327-354.

Millikan, Ruth. *Language, Thought, and Other Biological Categories*. MIT Press, 1984.

Moss, Sarah. "Right Reason in Plato and Aristotle: On the Meaning of Logos." *Phronesis*, vol. 59, 2014, pp. 181-230.

Okrent, Mark. *Nature and Normativity: Biology, Teleology and Meaning*. Routledge, 2014.

Paul, L. A. *Transformative Experience*. Oxford, 2014.

Paul, L. A. "What You Can't Expect When You Are Expecting." *Res Philosophica*, vol. 92, no. 2, 2015, pp. 149-170.

Philosophy Department, UNH, Accessed March 28, 2023 https://cola.unh.edu/philosophy.

Rawls, John. "Two Concepts of Rules." *The Philosophical Review*, vol. 64, no. 1, 1955, pp. 3–32.

Ritchie, Katherine. "The Metaphysics of Social Groups." *Philosophy Compass*, vol. 10, 2015, pp. 310–321.

Ritchie, Katherine. "Social Structures and the Ontology of Social Groups." *Philosophy and Phenomenological Research*, vol. 100, 2020, pp. 402–424.

Rouse, Joseph. "Normativity." *The Routledge Handbook of Philosophy of the Social Mind*, edited by Julian Kiverstein, Routledge, 2017, pp. 545–562.

Rouse, Joseph. "Practice Theory." *Handbook of the Philosophy of Science. Vol. 15: Philosophy of Anthropology and Sociology*, edited by Stephen Turner and Mark Risjord, Elsevier, 2007, pp. 630–681.

Ryle, Gilbert. "Knowing How and Knowing That: The Presidential Address." *Proceedings of the Aristotelian Society*, vol. 46, 1946, pp. 1–16.

Small, Will. "Ryle on the Explanatory Role of Knowledge How." *Journal for the History of Analytical Philosophy*, vol. 5, no. 5, 2017, pp. 57–76.

Small, Will. "The Transmission of Skill." *Philosophical Topics*, vol. 42, no. 1, 2014, pp. 85–111.

Stanley, Jason. *Know How*. Oxford, 2017.

Sterelny, Kim. *The Evolved Apprentice*. MIT Press, 2012.

Thomasson, Amie L. "The Ontology of Social Groups." *Synthese*, vol. 196, no. 12, 2019, pp. 4829–4845.

Witt, Charlotte. "In Defense of the Craft Analogy: Artifacts and Natural Teleology." *Aristotle's Physics: A Critical Guide*, edited by Mariska Leunissen, Cambridge, 2015, pp. 107–120.

Witt, Charlotte. *The Metaphysics of Gender*. Oxford, 2013.

Witt, Charlotte. "Norms." *Oxford Handbook of Social Ontology*, edited by Stephanie Collins et al., Oxford, forthcoming.

Witt, Charlotte. "What Explains Social Role Normativity?" *Social Functions in Philosophy*, edited by Rebekka Hufendiek et al., Routledge, 2020, pp. 122–135.

Young, Iris Marion. "The Five Faces of Oppression." *Geographic Thought: A Praxis Perspective*, edited by George L. Henderson and Marvin Waterstone, Routledge, 2009, pp. 55–71.

# Index

*For the benefit of digital users, indexed terms that span two pages (e.g., 52–53) may, on occasion, appear on only one of those pages.*

Afunctions. *See also* artisanal theory
   action and production
     distinguished in, 47–48
   biological functions contrasted
     with, 49–50, 55–57
   centrality of, 44
   complexity of, 61–62
   context-sensitivity of, 61
   definition of, 38, 49–50
   derivation of, 44–46
   distinctness compared to other
     functions of, 49–50, 54–57
   embedded nature of, 48–49, 62
   excellence and, 15, 38–39, 45–46,
     49–50, 118–19
   expertise and, 45–46, 55, 61
   flexibility of, 61
   identity and, 47
   intentions and, 50
   interconnected nature of, 62
   intrinsically normative nature of,
     45–46, 59–60
   key features of, 61–62
   locality of, 49
   noninstrumental nature of, 45–46,
     47–49, 54–55
   social science functions
     distinguished from, 49–
     50, 54–57
   techniques and, 38, 51
   terminology of, 38n.7

Anderson, Elizabeth, 1, 25, 42–43,
   68–69
Annas, Julia, 79, 88n.2
apprentice learning model, 89, 92–
   94, 112–13
Aristotle
   central examples used by, 47
   contemporary defenses of,
     50–54
   *eudaimonia* and, 45
   excellence and, 40, 45, 47–48
   expertise and, 54, 77–78, 95–96,
     98–99
   externalism and, 44, 52
   function argument of, 6–7, 40,
     44–48, 50–53
   habituation and, 89, 93, 94–96,
     98–99, 125
   imitation and, 95–96
   internalism and, 50
   know-how and, 77–78
   Plato's conception of
     function contrasted
     with, 46–47
   practical knowledge and, 74
   practices and, 52–53
   rationality and, 51–52
   social knowledge and, 54
   techniques and, 54, 73–74,
     79, 95–96
   virtue and, 79, 89, 95–96, 98–99

INDEX

artisanal theory. *See also* Afunctions
   critical selves and, 15–16, 51, 61, 80–83, 85–89, 91, 94–100, 126, 130
   definition of, 14–15, 43–44
   embeddedness of social roles in, 64–65, 119–20
   expertise and, 11, 14–16, 33–34, 44, 51, 57–58, 72, 78–79, 82, 87, 92, 96–97, 125–27
   explanatory advantages of, 61–65, 78–79, 91, 118–20, 131–34
   explanatory challenges for, 16–17
   externalism and, 9–10, 15–16, 27–28, 33–34, 38–39, 44, 66–68, 71, 102–3, 114
   gender and, 13, 116–17, 118–19
   habituation and, 11, 87–88, 94, 96, 112, 129–30
   holism of social roles in, 121–27
   internalism and, 33–34, 38–39
   key features of, 61–62
   know-how and, 51, 96–98
   know-why and, 11, 96–98
   methodological individualism and, 66–72
   nonreductive nature of, 11, 69–70
   overview of, 6–7, 17–18, 43–54, 131–34
   race and, 12–14
   rules-of-the-game explanation and, 57–65
   self-creation and, 16–18, 102–3, 111–15
   situatedness of social roles and, 118–20
   skill acquisition and, 89, 94, 98
   social agency and, 15–17, 101–2
   social coordination and, 38–39, 120–23, 127
   social ontology and, 66–71
   social positioning theory and, 62–65
   techniques and, 9–16, 27–28, 33–34, 44, 51, 68–69, 72, 82, 125–26, 127, 133–34
Ásta, 67

Barney, Rachel, 45
Bicchieri, Cristina, 23, 107
biological functions, 30, 49–50, 55–57
Brandom, Robert, 24–25
Brennan, Geoffrey, 25, 45n.3
Broadie, Sarah, 47–48, 96

Callard, Agnes, 101, 103, 107–11
coordination. *See* social coordination
critical selves. *See also* self-creation
   artisanal theory and, 15–16, 51, 61, 80–83, 85–89, 91, 94–100, 126, 130
   courage required for, 81–82
   eliminators and, 86–88, 101
   excellence and, 82, 93–94, 96–98
   expertise and, 78–79, 80–81, 87, 89–94, 96, 100
   externalism and, 81–82, 85
   gender and, 86–87
   habituation and, 78–79, 82, 87–88, 94–100
   internal criticism, 60–61, 93–94
   internalism and, 81–82
   know-how and, 87–88, 91, 94, 96–98
   know-why and, 78–79, 88, 96–97
   nonconformers and, 80–83, 85, 86–87, 100
   overview of, 80–83, 84–88
   reformers and, 86–88, 101
   skill acquisition and, 89–94
   social hierarchy and, 126, 130
   social roles and, 86–88, 101
   techniques and, 78–79
Cummins, Robert, 55

INDEX    141

Davidson, Lacey, 80
decision theory, 106–7
definitions
   Afunctions, 38, 49–50
   artisanal theory, 14–15, 43–44
   expertise, 76–77
   externalism, 9, 19, 26–27
   habituation, 94–96
   internalism, 8–9, 19, 22
   social normativity, 1–3, 40–43
   social roles, 6, 11–15, 41–42
   techniques, 73–74
Dreyfus, Hubert, 89–92, 94

eliminators of social roles, 86–88, 101
embeddedness of social roles, 48–49, 62, 64–65, 119–20
excellence
   Afunctions and, 15, 38–39, 45–46, 49–50, 118–19
   critical selves and, 82, 93–94, 96–98
   expertise and, 82, 87–88
   functions and, 40, 45, 47–48, 59–60
   habituation and, 11, 96–98
   know-how and, 11, 96
   know-why and, 96–97
   locality of standards for, 45–46, 49, 53–55, 118–20
   social hierarchy and, 129–30
expertise. *See also* know-how
   acquisition of, 78–79, 82, 89–94, 98, 125–26
   Afunctions and, 45–46, 55, 61
   apprentice learning model and, 89, 92–94, 112–13
   artisanal theory and, 11, 14–16, 33–34, 44, 51, 57–58, 72, 78–79, 82, 87, 92, 96–97, 125–27
   critical selves and, 78–79, 80–81, 87, 89–94, 96, 100

   definition of, 76–77
   excellence and, 82, 87–88
   externalism and, 33–34
   guided practice and, 82, 83, 87, 91–92, 98–99, 125, 129, 130
   habituation and, 87–88, 125
   know-why and, 78–79, 88, 91–92, 93–94, 97–98
   overview of, 76–80
   social hierarchy and, 125, 127
   social roles and, 12–14
   techniques, relation to, 6, 73, 77–78, 80
externalism
   arguments for, 29–32
   artisanal theory and, 9–10, 15–16, 27–28, 33–34, 38–39, 44, 66–68, 71, 102–3, 114
   complications for, 35–39
   critical selves and, 81–82, 85
   definition of, 9, 19, 26–27
   expertise and, 33–34
   explanatory advantages of, 81–82, 85
   forms of, 9, 26–29
   functions and, 28–29
   game theory and, 26–27
   gender and, 21–22
   methodological individualism and, 67–68, 71
   overview of, 9–11, 26–29
   rules-of-the-game explanation and, 62
   self-creation and, 101–3, 113–15
   social agency and, 15–17
   social ontology and, 67–68, 71
   social positioning theory and, 26–27
   techniques and, 27–28, 33–34

Fossheim, Hallvard, 95–96
Frye, Marilyn, 131–34

functions. *See also* Afunctions; techniques
  Aristotelian account of, 6–7, 40, 44–48, 50–53
  biological functions, 30, 49–50, 55–57
  excellence and, 40, 45, 47–48, 59–60
  externalism and, 28–29
  function argument, 6–7, 40, 44–48, 50–53
  internalism and, 30
  social science functions, 49–50, 54–57
  techniques and, 14–15, 51, 75

gender
  artisanal theory and, 13, 116–17, 118–19
  critical selves and, 86–87
  externalism and, 21–22
  habituation and, 98
  identity and, 31
  internalism and, 21–22, 31–32
  motherhood and, 106–8
  nonconformity to, 21–22, 86–87
  normative variability of, 118–19
  norm-relevancy account of, 31–32
  self-creation and, 106–8
  social hierarchy and, 114–15, 116–17, 127, 129
  as social roles, 12–14
*Gorgias* (Plato), 100
guidance conditions for self-creation, 110–11
guided practice, 82, 83, 87, 91–92, 98–99, 125–26, 129, 130

habituation
  artisanal theory and, 11, 87–88, 125–26, 130
  critical selves and, 78–79, 82, 87–88, 94–100
  definition of, 94–96
  excellence and, 11, 96–98
  expertise and, 87–88, 125
  gender and, 98
  guided practice and, 82, 83, 87, 91–92, 98–99, 125–26, 129, 130
  internalism and, 33
  know-how and, 11, 75, 82, 96, 112
  know-why and, 97–98
  overview of, 94–98
  punishment and, 98–99
  reward and, 98–99
  skill acquisition and, 89–94, 98
  social hierarchy and, 129
  techniques and, 74–75, 82, 88, 125, 127–29
  terminology of, 94–95
Hardimon, Michael, 11–12n.6
Haslanger, Sally, 67, 131–33
Hegel, G. W. F., 22–23, 24–25
Heidegger, Martin, 89–90, 114
hierarchy. *See* social hierarchy
holism of social roles, 121–27
Hume, David, 22–23, 24, 107

identity, 23–24, 31–32, 47, 117–18, 131, 132–33
imitation. *See* habituation
internalism
  arguments for, 33–35
  artisanal theory and, 33–34, 38–39
  challenges to, 23, 26
  collective agency and, 25
  complications for, 35–39
  conditional preferences and, 23
  critical selves and, 81–82
  definition of, 8–9, 19, 22
  as dominant approach, 29
  forms of, 8–9, 22–26

INDEX 143

functions and, 30
gender and, 21–22, 31–32
habituation and, 33
Hegelian account of, 22–23, 24–25
Humean account of, 22–23, 24, 107
Kantian account of, 22–24, 36
overview of, 8–9, 22–26
recognition forms of, 24–25, 36
self-creation and, 101–3, 107, 110–12

Jenkins, Katherine, 31–32

Kelly, Daniel, 80
know-how. *See also* expertise
artisanal theory and, 51, 96–98
critical selves and, 87–88, 91, 94, 96–98
definition of, 76–77
ethical know-how, 90–93
excellence and, 11, 96
habituation and, 11, 75, 82, 96, 112
intellectualism distinguished from, 76–77
knowing-that, relation to, 76–77
know-why and, 78–79, 88, 91–92, 96–98
modern debate on, 76–77
race and, 132–33
techniques and, 73–74, 78–79, 88, 133
know-that, 76–77
know-why
artisanal theory and, 11, 96–98
critical selves and, 78–79, 88, 96–97
definition of, 11
excellence and, 96–97
expertise and, 78–79, 88, 91–92, 93–94, 97–98
habituation and, 97–98
know-how and, 78–79, 88, 91–92, 96–98

self-creation and, 112
techniques and, 74
Korsgaard, Christine, 23–24, 50–52, 110–11

Lawson, T., 26–27, 62–65
locality of standards for social roles, 14–15, 45–46, 49, 53–55, 77–78, 118–20

MacIntyre, Alasdair, 50–51, 52–54
Mallon, Ron, 11–12
*Meno* (Plato), 89
Millikan, Ruth, 55

nonconformers to roles, 80–83, 85, 86–87, 100
noninstrumental norms, 45–46, 47–49, 54–55
nonreductionism, 11, 69–70
normativity. *See* artisanal theory; externalism; internalism; social normativity overview

Okrent, Mark, 113n.5
oppression. *See* social hierarchy
overviews
artisanal theory, 6–7, 17–18, 43–54, 131–34
critical selves, 80–83, 84–88
expertise, 76–80
externalism, 9–11, 26–29
habituation, 94–98
internalism, 8–9, 22–26
self-creation, 101–4, 114–15
social hierarchy, 116–18, 128–30
social normativity, 1–3, 40–43
social ontology, 66–72
techniques, 73–80

Paul, L. A., 106–8
Plato, 45, 46–47, 49–51, 55, 89, 100
proleptic reasons, 109–11

# INDEX

prudential norm view, 1, 3, 5–6
punishment, 3, 5–6, 98–99

race
   artisanal theory and, 12–14
   know-how and, 132–33
   social hierarchy and, 116, 118–19, 128, 129
   as social roles and, 12–14
Rawls, John, 60
reformers of social roles, 86–88, 101
regulism. *See* rules-of-the-game explanation
roles. *See* gender; race; social roles
Rouse, Joseph, 58
rules-of-the-game explanation, 57–65
Ryle, Gilbert, 76–77

self-creation. *See also* critical selves
   artisanal theory and, 16–18, 102–3, 111–15
   bait and switch and, 104–6
   decision theory and, 106–7
   examined life to success on Wall Street example of, 104–6
   externalism and, 101–3, 113–15
   gender and, 106–8
   guidance conditions for, 110–11
   internalism and, 101–3, 107, 110–12
   know-why and, 112
   motherhood example of, 106–8
   overview of, 101–4, 114–15
   paradox of, 83, 102–3, 108–15
   proleptic reasons and, 109–11
   revisiting paradox of, 111–14
   self-development distinguished from, 103–4
   transformation and, 106–8
skill acquisition, 89–94, 98
Small, Will, 74n.6

social agency, 15–17, 55–56, 101–2, 114, 116–17, 127
social coordination, 38–39, 53, 115, 120–23, 127
social hierarchy
   artisanal theory and, 116–19, 124–30
   critical selves and, 126, 130
   excellence and, 129–30
   expertise and, 125–26, 127
   gender and, 114–15, 116–17, 127, 129
   habituation and, 129
   holism and, 121–27
   nonhierarchical relations and, 116, 125, 126–27
   nonoppressive relations and, 116, 126–27
   normative oppression and, 124–25, 129–30, 131–34
   normative ordering and, 124–28
   overview of, 116–18, 128–30
   persistence of, 128–30
   race and, 116, 118–19, 128, 129
   social roles and, 124–28
   techniques and, 116, 125–26, 127–29
   transmission hierarchies, 127–29
social knowledge, 6, 11–12, 54, 73
social normativity overview
   applied ethics view, 3–6
   central puzzle of social normativity, 1, 11–12, 42–43
   definition of social normativity, 1–3, 40–43
   distinctness of social normativity, 3–6, 10
   prudential norm view, 3, 5–6
   realism, 3–6
   social roles, 2–3, 6–7
   source of normativity, 1–9, 10–13, 15–16

social ontology, 66–72
social positioning theory, 9, 26–27, 62–65
social roles. *See also* artisanal theory
   Afunctions and, 6–7
   conditions for social kind membership and, 20–21
   critical selves and, 86–88, 101
   definition of, 6, 11–15, 41–42
   embeddedness of, 64–65, 119–20
   expertise and, 12–14
   game theory and, 13–14
   gender as, 12–14
   ontology of, 11–15
   oppression and, 131–34
   overview of, 2–3, 6–7
   position and occupier distinguished in, 41–42, 72
   race as, 12–14
   rational choice theory and, 13–14
   situatedness of, 118–20
   social coordination and, 120–23
   social hierarchy and, 124–28
   social knowledge and, 6, 11–12
   techniques and, 7, 12–16
Sterelny, Kim, 89, 92–94, 96–97

techniques
   Afunctions and, 38, 51
   artisanal theory and, 9–16, 27–28, 33–34, 44, 51, 68–69, 72, 82, 125–26, 127, 133–34
   critical selves and, 78–79
   definition of, 73–74
   expertise, relation to, 6, 73, 77–78, 80
   externalism and, 27–28, 33–34
   functions and, 14–15, 51, 75
   habituation and, 74–75, 82, 88, 125, 127–29
   know-how and, 73–74, 78–79, 88, 133
   know-why and, 74
   overview of, 73–80
   social hierarchy and, 116, 125–26, 127–29
   social ontology and, 68–69
   social roles and, 7, 12–16
Thomasson, Amie, 12n.7
Trump, Donald, 40–41

virtue. *See* excellence

Wittgenstein, Ludwig, 58–60

Young, Iris Marion, 124